Trade Unions and Revolution

James Hinton and Richard Hyman

Trade Unions and Revolution

**The Industrial Politics of
the Early British Communist Party**

Pluto Press

First published 1975 by Pluto Press Limited
Unit 10 Spencer Court, 7 Chalcot Road, London NW1 8LH
Copyright © Pluto Press 1975

ISBN 0 902818 78 3

Printed by Bristol Typesetting Company Limited
Barton Manor, St Philips, Bristol
Design by Richard Hollis, GrR

Cover picture: Communist Party meeting,
Clapham Common, 1926. Fox Photos.

Contents

Abbreviations

AEU: Amalgamated Engineering Union
BSP: British Socialist Party
CI: Communist International/ Comintern
CP/CPGB: Communist Party of Great Britain
ECCI: Executive Committee of the Communist International
GC: General Council (of the TUC)
MFGB: Miners' Federation of Great Britain
MM: Minority Movement
NMM: National Minority Movement
NUGMW: National Union of General and Municipal Workers
NUGW: National Union of General Workers
NUR: National Union of Railwaymen
RILU: Red International of Labour Unions
SDF: Social-Democratic Federation
SLP: Socialist Labour Party
TGWU: Transport and General Workers' Union
TUC: Trades Union Congress

Revolutionary socialists are naturally interested in the history of the revolutionary movement, and study it expecting to learn lessons they can apply to their current practice. The growth of revolutionary politics in Britain and the increasing intensity of industrial conflict in recent years has generated interest in the early years of the Communist Party of Great Britain, the development of the Minority Movement, and the experience of the 1926 General Strike. If we are to learn the right lessons from these events, it is important that we should ask the right questions.

Historical writing about the early Communist Party is now quite extensive. The most valuable accounts, Macfarlane's history of the Party in the 1920s and Martin's history of the Minority Movement, are written from a frankly non-revolutionary perspective.[1] Both books are based on the correct assumption that, in Macfarlane's words: 'The history of the CP in the 1920s is the story of the struggle to forge a revolutionary party in a non-revolutionary situation.' Both works, however, over-react by treating the Party's revolutionary inheritance and pretensions as merely a 'false consciousness' resting on an inaccurate perception of the situation. The implicit assumption is that there is no point in being a revolutionary in a non-revolutionary situation. Consequently both authors treat their own evaluative standpoint as quite unproblematic: they assess the CP only in terms of its success as a militant reformist organization.

Others have taken this approach further. Walter Kendall, building on the ideas of the ex-Communist J.T.Murphy in his 1934 book *Preparing for Power*,[2] has argued that there was no genuine basis for the foundation of a Communist Party in 1920–21.[3] He presents the party and the ideology of communism as something artificially imposed on the British socialist movement. That movement, he argues, would have been far more effective had its personnel not organized themselves separately from the mainstream of working-class politics in the Labour Party. Whatever the value of this argument within a left reformist perspective, it is of little help if one is wanting to evaluate the early CP from a revolutionary standpoint. It is perfectly clear that the only alternative to the formation of a CP in 1920–21, was the fragmentation and complete ineffectiveness of the revolutionary left. One may certainly argue about what kind of CP should have been formed: but not, from a revolutionary standpoint, about whether the CP should have been formed at all.

There are two theoretical approaches to the early CP that claim to be revolutionary. The first is represented by James Klugmann's official history of the party.[4] Perhaps it is wrong to call this a theoretical approach at all. Klugmann's method is antiquarian. His evaluation seldom rises above minor organizational criticism. He never faces up to the question: by what criteria does one evaluate a revolutionary party operating in a non-revolutionary situation?

The second explicitly revolutionary approach fails in this respect too – because it is premised on the belief that the 1920s *did* present significant revolutionary possibilities to the British working class. This is the 'orthodox Trotskyist' approach developed by Brian Pearce and Mike Woodhouse (of the Socialist Labour League / Workers' Revolutionary Party), who focus on the Party's failure to capitalize on the crisis of the General Strike.[5]

The General Strike occurred at the height of the historic battle between Stalin and Trotsky. Naturally, post-mortems on the British strike became a major issue in the more general conflict within the world communist movement, second only in importance (in the international field) to the contemporaneous events in China. 'Trotskyist' writers have taken as the starting point of their own historical enquiry Trotsky's contemporary analysis of the strike, and in particular his attempt to blame the Stalinist bloc in the Communist International, for the British Party's failure to grasp 'whatever opportunities the situation offered to the revolutionary movement'. Hence it is concluded that 'the working-class paid and paid heavily for the debilitating influence of the Comintern'.[6]

The objections to this analysis are two-fold. Firstly it is untrue that the Communist International was pulling the CPGB to the right: almost always the CPGB itself stood to the right of the Stalinist majority in the International. Secondly the ritual assertion of missed revolutionary opportunity characteristic of this school is, in this instance, based on a cavalier disregard for genuine historical investigation of the real possibilities of the 1920s, the real balance of class forces, the real level of consciousness of the workers. The implication, all too clear, of this approach is that it is above all the 'voluntary' activity of the Party, not the broader and more 'determined' activity of the class, that itself creates the possibility of socialist revolution.

The viewpoint elaborated here differs in important respects from all those to be found in the existing literature on the early years of the Communist Party. Our argument, baldly stated, is that in the objective circumstances of Britain in the 1920s it was a mistake to attempt to construct a *mass* revolutionary party. On the criteria set out by the Communist International itself the situation could hardly have been less favourable for such an enterprise. In attempting to build a mass party, when it should have been concentrating on consolidating a small cadre, the Party sacrificed revolutionary clarity in its theory and in its propaganda to an illusory pursuit of growth at any cost.

Two disclaimers must be made at the outset. First, we are not attempting to provide a general history of the CPGB in the 1920s – but rather to present an interpretative perspective. Our conclusions are not grounded in the range and depth of original research that would be necessary to establish them firmly. Our intention, in publishing this essay, is as much to stimulate further research which may well modify many of our conclusions, as it is to indicate the weakness of previous attempts to evaluate the experience of the early CP from a revolutionary standpoint. Second, we have concentrated, almost to the exclusion of anything else, on the industrial activity of the Party. This is not because we believe that its activities among the unemployed, in local politics and in parliamentary elections were unimportant. (Indeed, one of the implications of our argument may be that, given the very limited possibilities on the industrial field, activity in these more marginal areas of the class struggle was of exceptional importance for a revolutionary party during this period.) Nevertheless, in the Communist International's own judgment – which we share – it is primarily in the industrial struggle that the opportunities for intervention by revolutionaries are to be sought, and it is a party's performance in relation to these opportunities on which it is primarily to be judged.

There is a further reason for this emphasis. What was, above all, novel about the Communist Party in the history of the British revolutionary movement, was its emphasis on the politics of industrial struggle. With the exception of the tiny Socialist Labour Party, no marxist group or party in Britain before 1920 had attempted to ground revolutionary politics in the industrial struggle. And whatever we have to say in criticism of the manner in which the CP set about this task, it nevertheless remains the case that the unification of the revolutionary movement within a party which saw its role primarily in relation to industrial struggle represented a very major innovation and advance for revolutionary politics in this country.

1.
The Background and the Problem

The Communist Party of Great Britain was formed during 1920 and 1921, the product of a painful series of negotiations between the various revolutionary parties and sects previously in existence.[7] The biggest component of the new Communist Party was the British Socialist Party, successor to the Social-Democratic Federation founded by Hyndman in the early 1880s; Hyndman, however, had seceded from the BSP with a pro-war minority in 1916. Traditionally SDF-BSP activity had focused on the politics of the street (open air propaganda, organizing the unemployed, etc.), and on municipal elections. The Party saw parliamentary elections as its main route of advance, though since its foundation in 1884 it had failed to win a single seat. Its attitude towards industrial struggle was negative in the extreme, although during the war it did number a few prominent industrial militants among its membership. The most notable of these was Willie Gallacher, Chairman of the Clyde Workers' Committee.

The second main component of the CPGB was the Socialist Labour Party (not all of its members – perhaps only a minority – took part in the merger). Originally a breakaway from the BSP, the SLP bitterly attacked its larger rival for opportunism and reformism. Central to SLP theory were the industrial unionist ideas of the American socialist Daniel de Leon, developed in Britain by James Connolly. From the outset, therefore, the SLP attached key importance to industrial activity. Despite its tiny membership (about 1,500 in 1919) the industrial orientation of the SLP made it an essential component of any united revolutionary party in 1920–21. It had been the chief political force within the wartime shop stewards' movement, and was to provide the CP with its most prominent industrial militants, men like Jack Murphy, Tom Bell and Arthur MacManus.

It is most unlikely that the small Marxist sects in Britain

11

would have come together into a united revolutionary party in 1920–21 without the mood of revolutionary optimism engendered by foreign events, and the direct interventions of the Communist International. Nevertheless revolutionary unity in Britain was rooted in domestic as well as foreign experiences. Above all, the Party should be viewed as an attempt to bring together and organize effectively the new stratum of working class 'rank-and-file' leadership thrown up by the industrial upheavals of the 1910–20 decade.

Those upheavals had added a new dimension to working-class leadership. What characterized the strike movements of 1910–20 was, above all, the unofficial strike. Most of the big stoppages between 1910 and 1918 were initiated by unofficial action, and settled by union executives anxiously attempting to reassert control over the more militant sections of their membership. This was less true of the strikes immediately after the war: by then the executives were more firmly in control.

Unofficial strikes demand and create unofficial, rank-and-file leaders. The generation of young trade-union activists that matured during the decade 1910–20 learned about trade unionism in unofficial strikes, and tended to see themselves as rank-and-file leaders *first*; as aspirants to full-time union office *second*. They learned that the full-timer, the professional trade-union leader – in so far as he was removed from everyday life in the workshop or the pit – was not to be trusted. He was, perhaps, a *necessary* evil: but he was to be handled with caution, kept at arm's length. The 1910–20 generation of militant rank-and-file leaders was the working class's answer to the process of incorporation; to the crystallization, during the same period, of a full-time, professional trade-union bureaucracy working in collaborative relationships with the employers and with the state.

Rank-and-file leaders need and develop ideologies to justify and reinforce their activities. It was their search for an appropriate ideology that constituted the fundamental dynamic of change in the British revolutionary movement in the decade preceding the formation of the Communist Party – the change from syndicalism to communism. In the wartime shop stewards' movement the ideology of the rank-and-file leader found its purest

12

expression. The movement was militant in its method, revolutionary in its goals. Above all else it formalized the activists' distrust of the trade-union bureaucrat. That he was necessary to negotiate truces with the power of capital was accepted. The revolution could not come all at once. But he could not be trusted either to squeeze the maximum advantage out of capitalism, or to lead the revolutionary offensive when the time for that arrived. So the shop stewards established Workers' Committees, an alternative leadership to that of the trade-union hierarchies. 'We will support the officials,' declared the Clyde Workers' Committee in 1915, 'just so long as they rightly represent the workers, but we will act independently immediately they misrepresent them.' After the war the shop steward leaders came to see the Workers' Committees as embryos of revolutionary Soviets, as the local organs of working-class state power. In the situation of a General Strike these Committees would seize the leadership from the national trade-union bureaucracy, the TUC or the Triple Alliance. It was essentially around this perspective that the Communist Party was formed in 1920–21.[8]

The conception of revolutionary politics that was crystallized out of the experience of the European working class at the early Congresses of the Communist International was one that would naturally appeal to the leaders of the wartime shop-stewards' movement. The early CI repeatedly emphasized that its conception of the revolutionary process was grounded in the existence of militant rank-and-file organization in the factories. In July 1924 the Fifth Congress of the Communist International declared:

'A communist party which has not succeeded in establishing a serious factory-committee movement in its country . . . cannot be regarded as a serious mass communist party. . . .'

The Congress was equally forthright about the need to reorganize the party on the basis of factory branches:

'There can be no talk of building a serious internally-solid mass communist party so long as it is not based on party cells in the factories themselves. This is not merely an organizational, but a serious political question. No communist party will be in a position to lead the decisive masses of the proletariat to struggle and to de-

13

feat the bourgeoisie until it has this solid foundation in the factories, until every large factory has become a citadel of the communist party.'[9]

We must look to these criteria of success in building 'a serious mass communist party' – criteria derived for the British leaders as much from their own previous experience as from the Theses of the Comintern – attempting to evaluate the industrial politics of the Party during the 1920s, and beyond.

It would be difficult to exaggerate the difficulty of the task that the Communist Party of Great Britain had set itself. Even before its foundation the conditions essential to success were being undermined. Within weeks of the armistice, the power of the shop stewards' movement in the workshops was being crushed by the high levels of unemployment consequent on the run-down in munitions production and the widespread victimization of known militants. At the peak of the depression in 1921 unemployment in engineering rose to 27 per cent. As early as 1920, an observer wrote: 'The unofficial shop stewards' movement is at ebb tide, because of the percentage of unemployed in the metal trades. The man at the gate determines the status of the man at the bench.'[10]

Soon it was a wry joke that the shop steward leaders of 1918 had become the unemployed leaders of the 1920s. The emasculation of the rank-and-file movement was succinctly stated by Jack Murphy, the leading theoretician of the wartime shop stewards, in a speech to the Fourth Congress of the Communist International at the end of 1922:

> In England we have had a powerful shop stewards' movement. But it can and only does exist in given objective conditions. These necessary conditions at the moment in England do not exist. How can you build factory organizations when you have 1,750,000 workers walking the streets? You cannot build factory organizations in empty and depleted workshops, while you have a great reservoir of unemployed workers.

Nor was this reversal of the trends of the previous decade confined to the engineering industry. From the end of 1920 the depression threw the trade-union movement as a whole onto the defensive. A brief post-war boom collapsed suddenly at the end

14

of 1920, and official returns showed 17·8 per cent of insured workers out of work by the summer of 1921. For the remainder of the 1920s the figure rarely fell below 10 per cent; while the crisis of the early 1930s raised the number of unemployed to three million, or 23 per cent. Wage rates were slashed – though this was to some extent offset by falling prices – and working conditions in many industries were under repeated attack. In such circumstances, trade-union membership took an almost inevitable tumble: numbers slumped from 8·3 million in 1920 to 5·6 million two years later, and by 1933 reached a low of 4·4 million.

In these conditions the tradition of rank-and-file self-activity built up during the previous decade was increasingly difficult to sustain. It is true that the depression did not, in the short term, put an end to militancy. The period was marked by a series of major strikes and lock-outs. In the three years 1919–21, disputes accounted for an annual average of 49 million working days. Excluding 1926, when a record 162 million working days were recorded in stoppages, the following ten years involved an average of $7\frac{1}{2}$ million working days – still a large number, measured against previous British experience.

Nevertheless the depression did decisively alter the character of strike activity, and of the opportunities it presented for revolutionaries to build a rank-and-file movement.

Table 1: British Strike Statistics: Annual Averages

	No. of strikes	Workers involved (thousands)	Striker-days (thousands)
1900–10	529	240	4,576
1911–13	1,074	1,034	20,908
1914–18	844	632	5,292
1919–21	1,241	2,108	49,053
1922–25	629	503	11,968
1926	323	2,734	162,300
1927–32	379	344	4,740
1933–39	735	295	1,694

The pattern of disputes was dominated by coal-mining. In the immediate post-war period the miners had put forward an ambitious programme of demands, including the nationalization of the mines, backed by the threat of direct action. But the miners' leaders, for all their left-wing rhetoric, were confused in both strategy and objectives; the support of the TUC was lukewarm; and the unions were easily outmanoeuvred by the Lloyd George government. In the years that followed, the miners were to pay dearly for their vacillation in 1919. In the autumn of 1920 there was a fortnight's national strike in support of demands for higher wages; this was called off on the basis of a temporary settlement. The dispute merely 'drained the accumulated strike funds of the miners without yielding any lasting gain'.[11] Five months later came the fiasco of 'Black Friday'. The economic depression had struck, and the government had abandoned its wartime controls of the mining industry. The owners lost no time in demanding drastic wage reductions; and the miners called on the aid of the railwaymen and transport workers, who had joined with them in 1915 to form the Triple Alliance. But the Alliance had proved unreliable in the miners' previous struggles, and many of its leaders – most notably J.H.Thomas of the NUR – had no stomach for a fight. On Friday, 15 April 1921, the other unions called off their plans for sympathetic strike action; the miners fought alone for three months, before conceding most of the owners' demands.

In 1923 the miners launched a campaign to win back the losses of the previous defeat, and in 1924 agreement was reached for improvements in wages. But the gains were short-lived, for a year later the owners announced the most vicious attack yet on miners' conditions. Plans for a new 'Industrial Alliance' were hastily drawn up; and the TUC itself offered the miners positive backing, threatening to place an embargo on movements of coal if the owners carried out their planned lock-out. Unprepared for a major industrial crisis, the government intervened: the industry was given a nine-month subsidy to allow the lock-out notices to be withdrawn, while a Royal Commission (the second on the industry since the end of the war) was appointed to investigate the issues. This temporary success was hailed by the trade-union movement as 'Red Friday'. But the sense of victory was short-lived. The Royal Commission endorsed the owners' demands for longer hours and lower wages, and its report was rejected by the miners. Lock-out notices were again issued in April 1926, and expired at the end of the month. Up to and beyond the last minute the TUC negotiated with the government in an attempt to reach a compromise – over the heads of the miners. But the Tory government, after nine months of preparation, was determined on a showdown; and the unions found themselves reluctantly committed to instructing solidarity action – now broadened into a General Strike.[12] Nine days later, on 12 May, the TUC leaders – terrified at the implications of the struggle they had unleashed – unceremoniously surrendered. The miners' lock-out lasted until the end of the year, when virtual starvation forced them also to surrender.

Other industries also experienced notable conflicts. In the metal industries there was a major strike of foundry workers in 1919; the 1922 engineering lock-out over 'managerial functions', which lasted two and a half months; and a series of stoppages in shipbuilding from 1922 to 1924. The railwaymen struck for nine days in 1919. In 1924 the building unions conducted their first national strike. In textiles there was a national dispute in 1921, and a further series between 1929 and 1932.

Yet the appearance of industrial militancy in the 1920s is in many ways misleading. From the onset of the depression, the *number* of stoppages recorded in each year averaged some 500 – only half the level of the previous decade. What pushed up the totals of striker-days was the occurrence of an unprecedented number of large-scale and protracted stoppages, often involving whole industries: and these were invariably *defensive* in character. Most of these occurred in the years 1921–23, when the sudden economic collapse brought a wholesale attack on wages and conditions. Thereafter the major disputes were far more concentrated industrially: in coal-mining in 1926, and cotton in 1929–33. In both cases the conflict was rooted in the painful readjustment of Britain's traditional export industries to their loss of dominance in international trade. But coal and cotton were not typical of British industry between the wars: the more widespread pattern, even before the General Strike, was one of relatively stable and pacific industrial relations. Even coal and cotton eventually accommodated to this pattern. In the twenty years from 1933 there was not one single official national stoppage in Britain, and the annual average of striker-days fell below two million.

The impact of economic depression on shop steward organization is relatively well documented; its more general effects on the rank and file are more open to dispute. Nevertheless, there are many indications that the implications for self-activity and militancy were extremely serious. At worst, the experience of unemployment, lock-outs and deteriorating conditions of work led to demoralization. At best, it resulted in an attitude of uncertainty and defensiveness. For those who remained in trade unions, the growing self-confidence and self-assertiveness of the previous decade was checked, leading to a new relationship of dependence on the union bureaucracies.

As union strength on the shop floor was eroded by unemployment and victimization, the focus of power and influence within the unions shifted upwards to the full-time officials. In consequence, the 1920s represented a crucial stage in the consolidation of British trade-union bureaucracy. This process was reinforced by two further factors. First, there was the sheer size of the major unions, which stemmed from the massive growth in membership between 1910 and 1920 (from 2·6 to 8·3 million) and the extensive movement towards amalgamation in the years 1910 to 1924. At the turn of the century the largest union with centralized control, the Amalgamated Society of Engineers, had less than 100,000 members; by 1920 there were a dozen unions larger than this, many of them substantially so. In general, size renders a union particularly prone to bureaucratization; and while the turbulent years before 1920 inhibited the consolidation of officialdom, the stabilization of union structure and industrial relations in the subsequent decade favoured official dominance in the major unions. It is particularly noteworthy that while union membership fell drastically during the 1920s, the number of full-time officials appears actually to have increased.[18]

A second important factor was the growth of national collective bargaining. Before 1914 the key level of collective bargaining in most industries was the district, and negotiations were open to considerable rank-and-file influence if not actual control. The war brought rapid rises in the cost of living, affecting all

18

parts of the country in a fairly uniform manner. In these circumstances, national wage bargaining developed; and at the end of the war the Whitley Reports encouraged the setting up of Joint National Councils in many industries. In engineering, where no such bodies were set up, the war produced a vast increase in Central Conferences on local claims, leading both sides to agree that wage movements should be settled on a national basis. During the depression, the Engineering Employers' Federation prevented any return to district bargaining over wages.

In short, by the 1920s, the national bureaucracy in many unions had acquired an important role as negotiators. But while the consolidation of bureaucratic control was a general feature of British unionism in the 1920s, the nature and extent of this process varied considerably from union to union.

Table 2: The Principal British Unions		
Union	Membership in thousands	
	1920	1930
Miners' Federation of Great Britain (MFGB)	1,011	511
Amalgamated Engineering Union (AEU)	423	191
National Union of Railwaymen (NUR)	458	327
Dockers' Union	103	–
Workers' Union	492	–
Transport & General Workers' Union (TGWU)	–	417
National Union of General Workers (NUGW)	439	–
National Union of General and Municipal Workers (NUGMW)	–	283

The most notable example of bureaucratic influence was provided by the general unions. The numerous tiny transport and labourers' unions of 1910, sharing between them less than 100,000 members, had grown particularly rapidly to a combined membership approaching a million and a half by 1920. A series of amalgamations in the 1920s consolidated their organization into the two giant general unions of today. The TGWU, formed at the end of 1921 by the amalgamation of the Dockers' Union with many smaller bodies of transport workers, did contain sections with a tradition of rank-and-file militancy in the docks and London transport. But its first secretary, Ernest Bevin, was able to achieve a dominant position in relation to his lay executive; and the union had a large staff of full-time officials, all appointed from above.[14] In 1929 the TGWU merged with the Workers' Union, which possessed a strongly entrenched central leadership and little tradition of rank-and-file activism.[15] The National Union of General Workers also possessed a long tradition of official dominance; there was a history of militancy in some areas, such as London, but this was outweighed by such areas as Lancashire, long controlled by Clynes. In the amalgamation which formed the NUGMW in 1924, conservatism was reinforced by the other two participants, the National Amalgamated Union of Labour and the Municipal Employees.[16]

In other unions the pattern was somewhat different. In the NUR, the wartime shop stewards' movement had been paralleled by the development of unofficial 'vigilance committees' which exerted considerable pressure on the official leadership; but their influence declined with the end of the war. The formal structure of the union encouraged strong central control: the national executive (nominally a 'lay' body, but effectively full-time) had extensive powers; national officials were elected for life; while the official committees at district level were very weak. The two main officials, Thomas and Cramp, had many years' experience in the union's leadership before becoming joint general secretaries at the end of the war, and were able to wield effective control throughout the 1920s. Industrial relations on the railways had in fact been stormy as a result of the railway companies' hostility to unionism, and the grievances resulting from wartime government control; but the Railways Act of 1921 'marked the beginning of a period of the closest co-operation between the union leaders and the railway companies'.[17] Thomas in particular became notorious as the most conservative leader of any major union.

The AEU, by contrast – formed by amalgamation in 1920 – had a strong tradition of decentralization and rank-and-file influence. The districts held considerable power; there were relatively few full-time officials; and all were subject to regular reelection. Yet here too there was some increase in central control. Brownlie, the president from 1913 to his retirement in 1930, held a powerful position throughout the 1920s, which was accentuated by the erosion of workshop organization and the replacement of district by national wage bargaining.[18]

The miners too had a strong tradition of decentralization: indeed the national body was merely a federation of autonomous local unions, many of them with a background of considerable rank-and-file militancy. Yet the Miners' Federation could justly be described as a 'fortress of bureaucracy'. The major districts were larger than most national unions (South Wales, Yorkshire and Durham each had well over 100,000 members in 1920). Policy-making delegate conferences, at area and national level, were dominated by full-time local agents who were elected for life, though militant branches were able to mandate their conference delegates. One consequence was often a 'right-wing leadership continually forced to pursue a "left" course which it did not in any way believe in, and which it consistently sabotaged'.[19]

Bureaucratic consolidation affected not only individual unions but also the central organization of the trade union movement. For half a century the Trades Union Congress functioned as little more than a talking shop and a clearing house for lobbying politicians about proposed legislation. It avoided any involvement in industrial disputes, which were considered the exclusive concern of individual unions; the title of its central body, the Parliamentary Committee, indicated the narrow focus of its concern; and it was administered by a part-time secretary. But from the latter half of the war there were important changes: additional staff were appointed, a committee structure was instituted, and in 1921 the Parliamentary Committee was replaced by the modern General Council. In 1923 the first full-time TUC secretary, Bramley, took office, to be succeeded two years later by his deputy, Citrine. Changes in the formal structure and personnel of the TUC were paralleled by a broadening in its functions. During the war the government, anxious for union co-operation in its industrial and economic policies, involved TUC representatives in a wide range of consultative and collaborative machinery. (It was partly the success with which union officialdom was thus domesticated that stimulated the growth of rank-and-file organization.) This wartime relationship led naturally to the TUC's new role of mediator between individual unions and the government in some of the massive post-war industrial disputes.[20] To some extent, these developments were the result of demands for a more powerful and effective TUC. The call for a 'general staff of labour' came in particular from militants and socialists, who recognized that a movement of sectional unions each jealously protecting its own autonomy was highly vulnerable to the growing concentration of capital. Conversely, the main opposition to more centralization within the union movement came from the most conservative and narrow-minded of officials. Nevertheless, one consequence of these changes was the creation of a trade-union super-bureaucracy, even more remote from rank-and-file control than the officialdom of individual unions.

To summarize this brief analysis of the trade-union background: the role of the union bureaucracy was more central to industrial relations than in any other period of British labour history. The contrast with the decade before 1920 could not be more marked. Then, British trade unionism passed through a phase of almost unprecedented turbulence; industrial militancy, often with left-wing political undertones, emerged more or less spontaneously from rank-and-file self-activity; in many cases such militancy was detached from the official structures of trade unionism, which were themselves in a state of flux. But by the 1920s the official structures had become consolidated, while the scope for rank-and-file initiative was severely curtailed by the changed economic climate. Yet this was precisely the climate in which the CPGB set out to build a mass party on the basis of rank-and-file self-activity in the workplace.

2.
The Communist Party in Industry
1920-29

Founding the National Minority Movement

In the summer of 1920, when hopes of a revolutionary outcome to the international post-war crisis still ran high, the Second Congress of the Communist International spelled out a threefold industrial strategy for the new Communist Parties.[21] First, communists should work within existing reformist unions to turn them into 'efficient organs for the suppression of capitalism'; second, they should build, lead and politicize factory committees; third, they should work to build a revolutionary trade-union international, the Red International of Labour Unions (RILU).

The Communist International insisted on the need *both* to work within the existing unions, *and* to build rank-and-file organization based on factory committees, independently of the reformist unions. The independent organization of the rank-and-file – in Britain exemplified in the wartime shop stewards' movement – was seen by the International as essential. Independent organization was needed 'to fight the counter-revolutionary tendencies of the trade-union bureaucracy, and to support the spontaneous direct action of the proletariat', the latter, if necessary, independently of reactionary trade-union officials. At the same time the establishment of the RILU, whose British Bureau was set up under J.T.Murphy in December 1920, was intended to provide a revolutionary alternative to the 'yellow' trade-union international based in Amsterdam. Subsequently the shop stewards' movement, by then a mere shell of its former self, was merged into the British Bureau of the RILU.

By 1922 it was clear internationally that the immediate revolutionary crisis had passed. The working class of Western Europe had suffered a series of disastrous political and economic defeats. At its Fourth Congress, held in November 1922, the CI reassessed its position. Capitalism had survived the period of revolutionary crisis and had entered a second period of partial and temporary stabilization; 'the conquest of power as an immediate task of the day is not on the agenda'. Previously, the task of the communist parties had been to provide the masses with independent leadership, leading the masses directly into a struggle for power based on factory organization and soviets, and bypassing the reformist trade unions if they could not be won to the revolutionary struggle. In the new situation, 'independent revolutionary action' was no longer on the agenda, and attention turned perforce to the problems of weaning the workers from their reformist leaders by degrees. Communist strategy must focus on united fronts with the reformists. Revolutionaries must recognize that they were merely a minority within the unions, and for the immediate future would remain so. There was no prospect, in the short term, of mounting a revolutionary struggle for power independent of the existing union leaderships. Consequently, while Communists should still attempt to build rank-and-file movements, they must attempt to lead these, and carry out specific agitations within the unions, not directly, but through a united front organization.

The implications of this strategy for the CPGB were spelled out by Lozovsky at the Fourth Comintern Congress:

> As far as Britain is concerned, we see clearly that it would be disastrous if the party were content to organize its forces only within its little Party nuclei. The aim here must be to create a more numerous opposition trade union movement. Our aim must be that our Communist groups should act as a point of crystallization round which the opposition elements will concentrate. The aim must be to create, to marshal, to integrate the opposition forces, and the Communist Party will itself grow concurrently with the growth of the opposition.

It was in pursuit of this objective that the CP took its major industrial initiative of the 1920s – the establishment of the National Minority Movement.

The Comintern adoption of united front tactics coincided with a period of turmoil within the CPGB.[22] The original party constitution provided for an orthodox branch structure and an executive elected on a divisional basis; this clearly contradicted the principles of democratic centralism, and in practice proved inefficient. Party membership fell from the 4,000 claimed in August 1920 to little more than 2,000 a year later; while there was an evident lack of co-ordination in the party's work, not least within industry. Critics led by Gallacher persuaded the Fourth Party Congress in March 1922 to appoint a Commission on Organization, excluding existing party officials and executive members. The Commission – composed of Palme Dutt, then a young newcomer to revolutionary politics, Harry Pollitt, a boiler-maker and former BSP member, and Harry Inkpin, brother of the party secretary and also ex-BSP – reported to a special Congress in October. It was agreed to reorganize the party on Leninist lines, in particular replacing branches by working groups controlled by a district committee, and restructuring the central executive. In early 1923, following pressure from the Executive Committee of the Communist International (ECCI), the 'Bolshevization' of the British Party was taken a stage further, to produce major changes in leadership. Pollitt took over primary responsibility for trade-union work; Gallacher and J.R.Campbell (another ex-BSPer from Clydeside) became joint secretaries of the British Bureau of the RILU; while Dutt was appointed editor of *Workers' Weekly*, the revamped party journal. Meanwhile ex-SLPers like Murphy and Bell, who had previously had particular influence over industrial policy, were eased into less powerful positions.

While these internal developments delayed the opening of a campaign for the Minority Movement, the Comintern policy in fact made good sense in terms of the earlier industrial perspectives of the CPGB – or at least of members with a BSP background. As a response to the serious losses of union membership, and in particular those which followed the engineering lock-out, the British Bureau of the RILU launched a series of 'Back to the Unions' conferences in the autumn of 1922. The resolutions were virtually identical with the programme to be adopted by the Minority Movement two years later: higher wages and shorter hours; support for the RILU; and the reorganization of British trade unionism. The latter was to involve 'the concentration of all local forces of the movement in the Trades Councils, the trans-

25

formation of the existing unions into powerful industrial organizations, the concentration of the fighting power of the whole movement in the General Council of the TUC'.[23]

Industrial unionism was a long-standing objective of revolutionaries, though those with any realism recognized that it could be only a long-term goal; the wartime shop stewards' movement in particular had emphasized that 'unity from below' would first have to be achieved. The other demands had been foreshadowed in 1919 and 1920, by sections of the BSP who had urged that the Triple Alliance should be broadened into a general staff of the labour movement which could act as 'the executive committee of the class struggle', and that the Trades Councils should be transformed into local organizing centres of the same struggle.[24] The CP had considerable influence in a number of Trades Councils, and from 1922 began actively to cultivate these, launching a series of annual National Conferences. The perspectives underlying this activity were stated by the British Bureau early in 1923:

> If we cannot under present circumstances, with the unemployed so badly organized, build up all-embracing Workshop Committees, we can at any rate by joint activities of the unions and the Trades Councils create powerful nuclei around which the masses will gather as organization amongst the unemployed improves.[25]

The demand for more power to the General Council was raised in the course of the engineering lock-out by Dutt, in his capacity as editor of *Labour Monthly*. It was taken up enthusiastically by Pollitt, a regular delegate from his union to the TUC. As co-ordinator of the small band of communist delegates at the TUC, he showed a particular concern with the mechanics of union decision-making from the branch to the General Council; and the aim of re-structuring the TUC fitted comfortably within this perspective, particularly against the background of the industrial timidity and theoretical bankruptcy displayed by the bulk of union officialdom at the 1922 and 1923 Congresses.

By the autumn of 1923, the campaign for a Minority Movement was formally opened. In August, Gallacher launched a series of propaganda meetings; a month later, *The Worker*

26

(edited by Campbell) carried the banner headline 'The Rank and File Must Build a Minority Movement':

> In every union the rank-and-file forces must be gathered 1) around a definite fighting policy, 2) around concrete demands for union consolidation and reorganization, 3) around the necessity for creating a new ideology amongst the union membership, 4) around the necessity of training and developing a new leadership to replace the old.[26]

The RILU, it was announced, was already engaged in establishing sectional minority movements for miners, railwaymen, engineers, boilermakers and building workers. The *Workers' Weekly* argued that the lack of direction shown by the TUC at its 1923 Congress proved the need for 'a vigorous national left-wing movement to make an end of the existing bureaucratic stagnation'. Such a united front would need to be based on 'a positive programme, and not a negative opposition'; and 'the simplest and most obvious rallying point' would be 'the views of the TUC itself'.[27]

The task of constructing the Minority Movement proceeded systematically. The leaders of the Comintern clearly found the pace too slow, but if the project was to involve genuine rank-and-file initiative, it could hardly have been much faster.[28]

The most significant area of the Party's industrial influence in the early 1920s had been the coalfields. In the crisis of 1921 the CP had urged vigorous resistance to the owners' demands, warned against the possibility of betrayal by the Triple Alliance leaders, and bitterly attacked this betrayal when it became a reality. Unofficial Reform Movements had existed in many areas before the formation of the CP, and one of the first achievements of the new party was to co-ordinate these within a National Miners' Reform Movement. Through this medium a vigorous campaign was launched for higher wages, shorter hours, and a single national union. Thus a firm basis existed for the campaign, initiated at the end of 1923, to create a Miners' Minority Movement. This was duly established at a national conference in January 1924, and the following month it launched its own newspaper, *The Mineworker*. The new organization achieved an immediate and major success when in March 1924 A.J.Cook was elected secretary of the Miners' Federation; Cook was a former Party

27

member who still identified with revolutionary politics, and received active support from the Miners' Minority Movement.

In engineering the Party had considerable influence in a number of districts, and its pressure for militant policies had some influence on the official stance of the AEU. The CP had played an important role in the 1922 lock-out, helping to stiffen up the AEU's stand, and using its organization among the unemployed to prevent blacklegging. On the railways, CP members had played a significant part in a rank-and-file campaign which led to the formulation of demands for 'all grades' increases. Among other unions, a notable intervention by the CP was its support for the unofficial dock strike of July 1923. This existing basis of activity and influence made it a comparatively simple task to establish Metal and Transport Minority Movements.

By April 1924 the groundwork had been sufficiently prepared for the British Bureau of the RILU to announce a summer conference to establish the National Minority Movement; for three years, it claimed, the RILU had urged a united front behind a new programme of demands, and now the logic of this demand had been accepted by a number of prominent union leaders.[29]

At the Sixth Party Congress in May, Gallacher as chairman reported on the progress of the campaign. Somewhat disingenuously, the role of the CP itself in initiating the formation of Minority Movements was played down; and in its resolution the party adopted the posture almost of a detached adviser, warning that the campaign to be successful would have to culminate in the creation of a national Minority Movement.

> The growing opposition movements now springing up in the leading trade unions, industries and the Labour Party, are the first expression of the concrete raising of the demands of the workers and of a definite challenge to the existing leadership. The CP welcomes these minority movements as the sign of the awakening of the workers. . . . [But] the various minority movements cannot realize their full power so long as they remain sectional, separate and limited in their scope and character. The many streams of the rising forces of the workers must be gathered together into one powerful mass movement which will sweep away the old leadership and drive forward relentlessly to the struggle for power.

28

The conference to establish this national movement, already convened by the CP through the British Bureau, was held on 23 and 24 August 1924. 270 delegates attended, claiming to represent 200,000 workers. The aims of the new organization were defined as follows:

> to organize the working masses of Great Britain for the overthrow of capitalism, the emancipation of the workers from oppressors and exploiters, and the establishment of a Socialist Commonwealth; to carry on a wide agitation and propaganda for the principles of the revolutionary class struggle, and work within existing organizations for the National Minority Movement programme and against the present tendency towards social peace and class collaboration and the delusion of the peaceful transition from capitalism to socialism; to unite the workers in their everyday struggles against the exploiters; to maintain the closest relations with the RILU.

The programme, discussed in detail, covered a range of economic, organizational, and political issues. First there were demands for a minimum wage of £4 and an increase of £1 for all workers; and for a 44-hour week and the abolition of overtime. Then came proposals for a restructuring of the trade-union movement: the formation of workshop committees, with representatives guaranteed against victimization; the affiliation of Trades Councils and the Unemployed Workers' Movement to the TUC, with representation on the General Council;* and a General Council with full powers to direct the activities of the unions, and under an obligation to Congress to use those powers. The political demands were for workers' control of industry; workers' control of the Labour government then in office, with working-class policies; repudiation of the Dawes plan on German reparations and a campaign against the danger of war (both issues were the focus of current CP agitation); and international trade-union unity (i.e. a united front between the Amsterdam and Moscow Internationals).

We shall have occasion below to note the tendency of the British Party throughout the early 1920s to overstress the possi-

---

* Outside the specific industries already mentioned, the Trades Councils and the unemployed movement provided the main areas of significant CP influence.

bilities of a united front with reformist trade-union leaders. It is however important at this point to stress that in 1924 neither the CI, nor the CPGB (in so far as it followed the CI lead) was guilty of so doing. Or at least, they were aware of the dangers of excessive dependence on reformist leaders, and at times strove actively to avoid this kind of relationship. There were indeed ambiguities in the position of both the CPGB and the CI, and we consider some of these below.

In a period of partial capitalist stabilization, as the International had recognized since 1921, a united front policy was necessary. But the emphasis was to be placed on building the united front from below, not on paper alliances with and between sections of the national trade-union bureaucracy. While the National Minority Movement demanded greater power for the General Council, and tried to establish a new Industrial Alliance of the Executives of the Miners, Engineers and Transport Workers, it by no means restricted its activity to mobilizing support for these objectives at trade-union conferences. Success for such a strategy would probably be counter-productive, just as the apparent success of syndicalist propaganda ten years earlier in promoting the Triple Alliance had proved counter-productive. All power to the General Council meant all power to the executives, and the executives were more likely to use this power to crush militancy than to lead it – as they had already done through the Triple Alliance. The only way to ensure that a powerful General Council did not become a brake upon the movement was to demand at the same time the democratization of the General Council, and, above all, to take the initiative in developing the organization, self-activity and class consciousness of the trade-union rank-and-file in the localities. To this end the National Minority Movement coupled the slogan of all power to the General Council with campaigns for the formation of factory and pit committees. They pressed for the restructuring of the ineffective Trades Councils to make them directly representative of the workers in the factories and thus capable of becoming a real general staff for the whole of the local working class in a situation of crisis. And they demanded the direct representation of such Trades Councils at the TUC.

Given the existing relation of forces within the movement, and in particular the difficulty of building self-reliant rank-and-file organization able to take the initiative in mass action under conditions of high unemployment, the CP recognized the need for an alliance with the left wing of the trade union bureaucracy. The influence of that left wing was significantly increased by the departure from the General Council in 1924 of prominent right-wingers to serve in the first Labour Government. The Fifth Congress of the International had been clear on Communist attitudes towards this left trade-union bureaucracy, whose influence was most clearly revealed in the TUC's initiative for a rapprochement between the social-democratic Amsterdam International and the communist Red International of Labour Unions. This left was 'formless and politically vacillating'; it sought to reconcile reformism and communism – clearly an impossible task. The degree to which this left could be stiffened up and brought to a revolutionary position depended primarily on the strength of the independent rank-and-file minority movement led by the CP. The left trade-union leaders were to be judged, not merely on their attitude to international trade-union unity, but on their relationship with this rank-and-file movement and its struggles. 'The Comintern and the communist parties support the left-wing in so far as it really fights against the programme of the Amsterdam International. To overestimate the left wing, to ignore its timidity and inconsistency would be a grave error. Communists and the trade-union organizations they control must propose to the left wing ... the formation of joint committees of action. ... Communists must demand of the right wing ... who say that an (international) understanding ... is desirable, that they put these proposals into action in every country in the daily struggle. ...'[30]

When the National Minority Movement was formed the CP followed the Comintern lead. J.R.Campbell wrote in October 1924: 'It would be a suicidal policy for the CP and the Minority Movement to place too much reliance on the official left wing. It is the duty of the Party and the Minority Movement to criticize its weakness relentlessly and endeavour to change the muddled and incomplete left-wing viewpoint of the more progressive leaders into a real revolutionary viewpoint.[31] To achieve this the

31

Party must, while keeping the lines of communication open to the trade-union bureaucrats, concentrate its energy on building up the rank-and-file movement: on their attitude to this movement the lefts would be judged. In particular the limited significance of the lefts' support for the Anglo-Russian Trade Union Committee (established during the winter of 1924–25) was recognized: 'Unity that only means a polite agreement between leaders is useless unless it is backed up by mass pressure. Unity that confines itself to negotiations between Amsterdam and the Russian Unions only touches the fringe of the question. . . . The class struggle cannot be limited to an exchange of diplomatic letters.'[32]

The Party and the 'Left' Trade Union Officials

It is undoubtedly true that, during 1925–26, the CP failed to apply this line consistently in its propaganda, and therefore failed to prepare the very large numbers of workers within the orbit of the Minority Movement for the capitulation of the lefts during the General Strike. Little distinction, for example, was drawn between A.J.Cook, the Miners' General Secretary, who was willing to a large extent to identify himself with the Minority Movement, and the other left wingers on the General Council whose leftism amounted to little more than support for international trade-union unity, and who remained aloof from the Minority Movement.* Well before the General Strike the unreliability of these lefts was apparent. The Minority Movement was well represented at the Scarborough TUC in September 1925, and a number of important left-wing resolutions were passed, dealing with imperialism, international trade-union unity and the need to establish workshop committees. The official left wing were, however, almost wholly silent for much of the conference, leaving the Minority Movement delegates to do the fighting; and the leftist influence in the General Council was substantially

---

* Notably the ex-CP member Alf Purcell of the Furnishing Trades Association; George Hicks (Bricklayers); Alonzo Swales (AEU); and John Bromley (ASLEF). The last three of these were on the TUC committee charged with liaising with the miners during 1925-26, but the committee did nothing to ensure that adequate preparations were made for the strike.

32

undermined by the return of the right wingers, Thomas, Bevin, and Bondfield. As Trotsky was quick to point out, the left wing were all right on international questions since these had always been 'the line of least resistance for the "leaders". Regarding international matters as a means of giving vent to the radical moods of the masses, these esteemed leaders are prepared to a certain extent even to bow to a revolution (in other countries) . . .', and again: 'It should be understood that leftism of this kind remains left so long as it has no practical obligations. But as soon as the question of action arises, the left wingers respectfully concede the leadership to the right.'[33] The timidity and powerlessness of the official left was again revealed a few weeks later when the Labour Party conference at Liverpool decided to debar Communists from holding individual membership of the party; or from acting as trade-union delegates to party conferences.

The CP was well aware of the failures of the left-wing bureaucrats, but it saw no reason to break up the united front policy. After all it had always expected the lefts to be weak and vacillating, and when they proved to be so the logical thing to do was to step up the campaign to hold them on course by pressure from below. One aspect of this was clearly that the Minority Movement should demand the implementation of the Scarborough resolution on workshop committees, exhort the General Council to make adequate preparations for the anticipated crisis, and in particular press for a special conference of trade-union executives to give the Council the power it had declined at Scarborough to call and co-ordinate a General Strike.

This policy was sound – so far as it went. But the reaction to the evident unreliability of the trade-union 'lefts' was inadequate and confused. Thus in March 1926, when Swales and Hicks apparently supported a General Council decision not to call a special conference to prepare for the Strike, the Party attacked the decision but failed to call attention to the role of the so-called 'lefts'. Nothing reveals more clearly the confusion of the CP leadership on this question than the way the views of J.T.Murphy – one of the most clear-sighted of the Party's industrial leaders – oscillated during the run-up to the strike. In September 1925, analysing the lessons of Red Friday, Murphy had implicitly recognized the danger that the left wing of the trade-union leadership would capitulate to the right as soon as the real action started:

> Let us be clear what a general strike means. It can only mean the throwing down of the gauntlet to the capitalist state, and all the powers at its disposal. Either that challenge is only a gesture, in which case the capitalist class will not worry about it, or it must develop its challenge into an actual fight for power, in which case we land into civil war. Any leaders who talk about a general strike without facing this obvious fact are bluffing both themselves and the workers.[84]

This important analysis was not carried further; nor was it taken from the party's theoretical journal into its mass-circulation agitational press. Instead, two days before the strike actually started, Murphy wrote in the *Workers' Weekly*:

> Those who are leading have no revolutionary perspectives before them. Any revolutionary implication they may perceive will send the majority of them hot on the track of a defeat. Those who do not look for a path along which to retreat are good trade-union leaders who have sufficient character to stand firm on the demands of the miners, but they are totally incapable of moving forward to face all the implications of a united working-class challenge to the State.

Yet on his own previous argument, there was no middle way between surrender and revolution; it was possible to 'stand firm' only by 'moving forward'. The 'good trade-union leaders', just as surely as the reactionaries, were 'bluffing both themselves and the workers'.

On one analysis, a minority of union leaders were reliable. On the other, none were to be trusted. Yet in between presenting these rival interpretations, Murphy could denounce any attempt to set up *independent* Councils of Action at local or national level: 'there should be no rival body to the Trades Council. . . . We should avoid rivalry and recognize the General Council as the General Staff of the unions directing the unions in the struggle.'[35] Hence on one view, the miners could be defended only by civil war; on the second, a struggle guided by militant union leaders might suffice; on the third, the existing General Council as a whole could prove adequate to the task. Unable to

34

choose between these conflicting perspectives, it is not surprising that the party gave no clear lead in the run-up to the General Strike.

The Party and the International

How is this confusion to be explained?

Towards the end of 1924, Stalin began to develop the international implications of 'socialism in one country', attacking Trotsky for his 'infatuation' with the idea of the necessity for revolutions in the West. Trotsky, he argued, underestimated the effectiveness of the 'moral support' already given by the workers of Western Europe to the Soviet State as a barrier against renewed imperialist intervention.[36] This was the germ of the Stalinist policy of focusing attention on the value of the Anglo-Russian Trade Union Committee for the defence of the Soviet Union, at the expense of encouraging the Communist Party of Great Britain to develop its own independent revolutionary strategy. In line with ECCI policy the CP conference of May 1925 declared that it could give 'no countenance to the revolutionary optimism of those who hold that we are on the eve of immediate revolutionary struggles'. Over the next critical year the propaganda of international unity, and the associated restraint in criticism of the official left, took precedence over the propaganda of independent revolutionary initiative in the party press. It is the essence of the 'orthodox Trotskyist' case that the victory of Stalin within the International was *the main cause* of the CP's right opportunism during 1925–26.

If this were so, one would anticipate that any conflicts that occurred between the British Party and the International during 1925–26 would have been conflicts in which the CP stood to the left of the Comintern as it painfully adjusted itself to the new perspectives imposed from Moscow. But exactly the reverse is the case. Time and again the British Party was in trouble with Moscow for deviating to the right, not to the left, of the Stalinist line. For example, in September 1925 the Comintern expressed concern about the CPGB's tendency to relax party discipline over members elected to trade-union office, and reaffirmed the principle that such members were 'responsible for their work solely to the

35

Party'. The CP seems to have accepted this in a purely formal way: George Hardy, the Acting Secretary of the Minority Movement, continued to advocate 'a certain amount of freedom' to party members elected to trade-union office.[37] More important and significant was the divergence of opinion between the Comintern and the Party immediately before the General Strike. J.T.Murphy, as we have seen, expressed confidence in the ability of the official left to 'stand firm on the demands of the miners'. At the same time, while pointing to their incapacity as revolutionary leaders, he implied that this was not a matter of immediate concern since there was really no prospect of the strike developing into a revolutionary confrontation. This was consistent with the line the British delegates at the ECCI plenum in March 1926 had taken, when they criticized the official resolution on Britain for underestimating the 'immense resources and powers of resistance' still available to the British ruling class.[38]

Compare Murphy's analysis with the statement made five days earlier by the Executive of the International:

> A strike by the miners would imply a general strike, and a general strike cannot remain an industrial struggle. It is bound to develop into a political struggle. . . . The British bourgeoisie . . . will mobilize the entire power of the State, because the basic question of capitalist society will be raised, the question of private property. . . . The fight for wages and conditions will raise before the working class the question of power. [The statement went on to warn the working masses that the leaders were irresolute, and some were prepared to betray the fight before it had even begun.] Even the left-wing leaders of the Labour Party and the unions are showing themselves unequal to the situation. . . .

Again, when the strike was in progress Comintern instructed the Party that 'as the struggle develops, the party's slogans must be carried to a higher level, up to the slogan of the struggle for power.'[39] Thus the International stressed both the revolutionary possibilities of the strike, and the inadequacies of the official lefts which the CPGB ignored or denied. Such evidence is hardly consistent with a picture of right-wing pressures from Moscow being the main cause of the CPGB's reluctance to take a revolutionary initiative. The same is true of Comintern-Party relations immediately after the strike. While the skeleton Central Committee of the Party at King Street during the strike had sharply attacked the official left when their sell-out became unmistakable at the end of the nine days, the full Central Committee, meeting shortly after, and the leadership of the Minority Movement, toned down this criticism substantially. Probably the main consideration in their minds was a desire to maintain their links with the 'lefts' even now in order to facilitate mobilizing support for the miners' lock-out. In so far as they were motivated also by a desire not to embarrass continuing Russian support for the Anglo-Russian Committee they must have been surprised by the Comintern's sharp criticism of their attitude. J.T.Murphy, the Party's delegate in Moscow at this time, hotly contested the right of the Russian Trade Unions to attack publicly the British trade-union left.[40] It is of course true that Stalin's insistence on the contradictory policy of simultaneously attacking the lefts and professing faith in the future of the Anglo-Russian Committee was deeply confusing for the CPGB. It is, however, equally clear that in this instance, as previously, the British Party found itself to the right, not to the left, of the International.

In the light of this evidence the most that can be argued is that the right opportunism of the Comintern from 1925 allowed the British Party to abandon a revolutionary position that had previously been imposed on it by the Comintern. Much of Trotsky's own criticism of the British Party and his insistence on the need for a more positive lead from the International if the party was to develop at all would also point to this conclusion. But if this is the case, then it is absurd to see in the Stalinist obsession with the Anglo-Russian Trade Union Committee anything more than a secondary cause of the Party's rightist tendencies. The root cause is to be found within the Party itself and its domestic situation.* This is most clearly indicated by the fact

---

* An alternative explanation for the confusion of the CP leadership in the run up to the General Strike is to be found in the arrest and imprisonment of the most prominent leaders in October 1925. To the extent that the Party was so dependent on a small number of leaders, this would only serve to illustrate the political and theoretical weakness of the British Party.

that in 1925–26 the CP moved even further to the right than did the Comintern. As an explanation of the CP's failures in 1925–26, then, the 'orthodox Trotskyist' analysis is clearly inadequate.

The basic error of 'orthodox Trotskyist' analysis lies in its uncritical acceptance of Trotsky's contemporary belief that the British Party was operating in a potentially revolutionary situation. Mike Woodhouse's articles are presented as a review of Macfarlane's history of the CP, and the premise of his criticism of Macfarlane is a rejection of the latter's assumption that he was writing about 'the struggle to forge a revolutionary party in a non-revolutionary situation'. Against this Woodhouse posits a picture of a working class held back from revolutionary endeavour only by the inadequacies of the Communist Party. 'Far from their being in a non-revolutionary situation, the working class looked for a leadership that would give conscious expression to their objectively revolutionary aspirations.'[41] So long as one can blame the Comintern for the performance of the Party, one can avoid questioning the truth of this assumption. If however the main causes of the Party's rightist tendency appear to have been domestic, one is forced to question the truth of Woodhouse's assumption. Was it perhaps the objective British conditions in which it operated that pulled the Party rightwards? Is it not possible that Macfarlane's standpoint is after all right – that there was not a revolutionary situation in 1924–26? The most amazing feature of all the 'Trotskyist' writing is its complete failure to examine this possibility: it contents itself with the merest assertion.

The Comintern leadership did not disagree with Trotsky's basic argument that from 1924 the British working class was recovering its combativity after the profound demoralization wrought by Black Friday, the defeat of the Engineers in 1922 and the very high levels of unemployment of the early '20s. The growth of the Minority Movement, the Anglo-Russian Committee, the mobilization before Red Friday, the considerable support won by the CP in the Labour Party following the Liverpool Annual Conference decision to expel individual Communists –

all these were held by the Comintern to show that British workers were moving to a more revolutionary position. Underlying this was the experience of the 1924 Labour Government in first raising the hopes of the masses, and then exposing to 'the active minority of the labour movement' the worthlessness of reformism. Above all the decline of British imperialism, the consequent economic dislocation and chronic unemployment, and the ruling class's inescapable need to arrest this decline by cutting wages and lowering the standard of living, combined, it was argued, to produce an objectively revolutionary situation in Britain. Trotsky carried this analysis further, arguing that it was inconceivable that the British would peacefully surrender their supremacy to the United States, and predicting over the next two or three years a series of acute crises, of which the conflict over wages would be only a precursor (a 1905 for the Party); the crises would swell quite possibly into full scale war with the United States and the sudden and catastrophic collapse of the Empire.[42]

It would be interesting to go into the reasons why Trotsky's analysis, though in many ways an extremely perceptive one, was incorrect, but these matters lie outside our present discussion. It is only necessary to outline what Trotsky had in mind when he predicted a revolutionary situation in Britain to show how foolish it would be for us, knowing what we do, to accept uncritically Trotsky's analysis of the significance of the General Strike. Curiously enough none of our 'orthodox Trotskyists' mention Trotsky's own delineation of the British future.

The clearest evidence that there was not a revolutionary situation in 1924–26, despite the rising militancy of the workers, is to be found in the failure of the Minority Movement to achieve its most important original purpose – the construction of a powerful independent rank-and-file movement led by the Party, the united front from below. The 'Trotskyist' argument, of course, explains this as a result of the CP's over-dependence on the official left wing. Undoubtedly the tone of CP propaganda during 1925–26 was not such as to emphasize the extreme urgency of the need to construct effective rank-and-file organization. It is however, equally obvious (and entirely unconsidered by the 'Trotskyists') that an inability to construct independent rank-and-file organization, due to objective difficulties, could itself explain the Party's over-dependence on the left trade-union bureaucracy. How are we to decide? There is, in our view, considerable evidence to suggest that it was the objective difficulty of creating an independent rank-and-file movement, capable in a crisis and under CP leadership of seizing the initiative from the trade-union lefts, that caused the Party to moderate its criticisms of the left bureaucrats, rather than vice versa.

The CP and the National Minority Movement never abandoned their attempts to establish factory committees, or to restructure the Trades Councils to serve as local general staffs for the working class.[43] The National Minority Movement urged the General Council to implement the Scarborough TUC resolution which called for the formation of factory committees. More important, its press also carried articles calling on readers to take their own initiative in establishing factory committees and pit committees. Similarly at the National Minority Movement conference held in March 1926, which was devoted to the problem of 'preparedness', the Party was not content with suggestions to 'ginger up' the official leadership. The Conference was concerned to establish Councils of Action in the localities, and during the weeks that followed, the Movement, without waiting for initiatives from the General Council, circularized all Trades Councils urging them to call 'Conferences of Action for the purpose of setting up Councils of Action under the control and auspices of the Trades and Labour Councils'. These Councils were to be representative of all local working-class organizations, industrial, political and organizations of the unemployed: they were to make arrangements for food distribution during the anticipated crisis, arrange demonstrations and propaganda in support of the miners, and (an interesting priority) persuade women not to blackleg.[44] At the same time the Minority Movement was circulating a pamphlet describing a model constitution for 'Militant Trades Councils'. In the locality whose history during the Nine Days has been most intensively studied, the North East coast, the CP (in the person of Page Arnot) had an extremely detailed and precise plan of organization and action ready on the eve of the strike, a plan that was rapidly adopted by the Newcastle Council of Action and helped the North East to go further than most other areas towards checkmating the Government's efforts to keep control of food distribution during the strike.[45] In addition, while insisting that in the interests of unity the Councils of Action should accept the authority of the General Council, the National Minority Movement did not fail to point out that the right-wing majority on the General Council might back down. In the final issue of the *Workers' Weekly* before the strike began Tom Wintringham urged that in this not unlikely eventuality the local Councils of Action should immediately convene a national conference to take over from the General Council, and that delegates should at once be appointed ready to do this when the need arose.

Though the Party attempted during 1924–26 to establish factory committees, to remake the Trades Councils on the model of the wartime Workers' Committees, its efforts very largely failed. Similarly with factory branches: these were a key objective since the 'Bolshevization' of the Party in 1922–23, its transformation from the local propagandist structure characteristic of previous British revolutionary organizations to the functional, cell structure appropriate to an *interventionist*, vanguard party. It was easier to grasp the necessity of factory branches than actually to establish them. It was all very well for the Comintern to say that 'The main obstacle in the way of the formation of factory nuclei is the workers' fear of dismissals.' But the fear was grounded in hard experience, and the International's demand for 'a systematic ideological campaign' to remove this obstacle was hardly germane.[46] What use was ideology against the brute fact of victimization, against the crowd of unemployed outside the gate waiting for the foolish communist's job? Despite persistent pressure from the International, pressure that by no means tailed off during 1925–26, the CP had by the spring of 1926 only managed to get 17 per cent of its 6,000 members organized into factory cells, an increase of only 7 per cent over the previous year.[47] Objective conditions defeated the Party. Despite its own efforts and the Comintern's concern it was simply not possible in British conditions in the mid-1920s to build the type of party and the type of relationship with the masses that the Fifth Congress had rightly seen as the precondition of serious revolutionary politics.

The Party and the General Strike

There are circumstances in which a self-avowedly revolutionary party can be seen to act as a brake upon the development of the revolutionary movement. France in 1968 is an example of this. The crucial evidence of the French Communist Party's reactionary role in 1968 is that large sections of the striking workers moved well in advance of the Party, and that the Party responded not (like the Bolsheviks in 1917) by running to catch up with and get one step ahead of them, but by seeking to use its power to suppress their initiatives, to deny their ambitions. Great though the determination to stand by the miners was in 1926, there is no evidence that any significant section of British workers acted or thought much in advance of the Communist Party.

Left-wing optimists usually cite the General Strike as a magnificent example of the capacity of the working class spontaneously to throw up organization and leadership appropriate to their situation. In many respects it was. Since the General Council made virtually no effort to prepare for the strike, and since it did its best to restrict the development of effective local organization – Councils of Action – during the strike, all that was achieved in this line was a product of local initiative. The General Council sought to limit the Trades Councils' role to that of supporting the strike committees of individual unions, so as to maintain the vertical, sectional chains of command. In practice, in many areas, the strike committees merged into the Trades Councils (though never to the exclusion of accepting orders from above). To some degree, expanding their membership by accepting delegates from local political parties, co-op organizations, etc, the Trades Councils became an effective local general staff of the movement.[48] Such Councils of Action, in the most militant areas, established considerable power during the nine days. Mass pickets gave them control of the roads and thus of transport. The most sophisticated local plan of action – that drawn up by Page Arnot for the Newcastle Council of Action – was quite clear on the potential significance of this control:

> Whoever handles and transports food, the same person controls food; whoever controls food will find the 'neutral' part of the population rallying to their side. Who feeds the people wins the Strike.[49]

On Tyneside – where things went furthest – the Council was sufficiently powerful to call forth, and then reject, proposals from the local Government Commissioner for joint control of the movement of food supplies from the docks.[50] It was all very exciting – and very easy to misread. It looks like the embryo Soviet of Murphy's 1919 conception – but it was not.

Despite the plausibility of 'who feeds the people wins the strike', Page Arnot's slogan was not in fact the main issue in the General Strike. It would only have become so in a situation of civil war. The real issue of the strike had two aspects:

a. that to defend the miners it was necessary to overthrow the Government;
b. that none of the existing leadership of the trade-union movement had any intention whatsoever of overthrowing the Government through industrial action.

This was true not only of the General Council – right and left – but also of the great majority of the local trade-union officials who actually played the key part in running the strike, *and* indeed of the mass of the strikers themselves. Of course, it is urged, the consciousness of the mass of the workers could change very rapidly indeed in the actual experience of a general strike. No doubt it could, in specific situations. But there is little evidence that it did in May 1926.

The Councils of Action often revealed an impressive capacity for improvisation. But, if we compare them with the Comintern model, or even with the Workers' Committees of the First World War, it is clear that they were *not* embryonic soviets.

The General Council was bound to capitulate. Where was the alternative leadership? The evidence suggests that the bulk of that stratum of working-class leaders who ran the Councils of Action and the strike committees – the local trade union officials – were incapable of throwing off the discipline of the national trade unions, of defying the instructions of their executives. Consequently any effort to prolong the strike, or to carry it beyond its purely defensive objectives, would have required the emergence of a new leadership, a leadership based in a putative transformation of rank-and-file consciousness wrought by the experience of

43

the strike itself. Page Arnot claims that it was precisely this conception that lay at the basis of his plan of action – though it could not of course be spelled out in the hearing of the trade union officials with whom, of necessity, he was working:

> The intention was that the setting up of Councils of Action would enable the whole theatre of war from Tweed to Tees to be covered with a network of local Councils. From these would arise a more revolutionary leadership, as things developed, than was possible from the ranks of local or district officials of trade unions (who, however, found themselves constituted as the leaders of their members called out on strike).[51]

And he records, sadly: 'This stage was never reached. . . .' The alternative leadership could not be created overnight. In the North East the workers' solidarity was contained within the reformist structures of trade unionism. The Council was not a unified class organization, not an embryonic soviet, but a forum for negotiation between the sectional interests of the local trade-union bureaucracy.[52]

There seems to be no evidence that any section of workers attempted to move beyond this structure and all that it implied in terms of the limitation of the struggle to defensive demands. Nothing comparable to the direct democracy characteristic of the First World War Workers' Committees occurred.[53] The striking workers were not able or willing, as the engineers had been during the First World War, or as many workers are today, to declare their independence of reformist trade unionism: 'We will support the officials just so long as they rightly represent the workers, but we act independently immediately they misrepresent them.' Similar conclusions arise from a study of Liverpool during the strike, despite Merseyside's tradition of spontaneous and unofficial class uprisings.[54] The working class was far from being, as Woodhouse asserts, poised on the brink of dual power, of a struggle for soviet power. There is good reason to believe that, had the CP attempted to politicize the struggle by raising the demand for 'All Power to the Councils of Action', the slogan would have fallen even flatter than did its demand for nationalization of the mines and a General Election. Far from being 'anachronistic' in a 'situation of dual power',[55] even this slogan would appear to have

44

been more than one step ahead of the actual ambitions of the strikers.

Had the strike occurred as the culmination of a period of trade-union advance, a period in which rank-and-file self-activity had thrown up a rank-and-file leadership – in 1919 for example – the outcome might have been very different. But that is precisely why it did not occur in 1919. In 1919 Cabinet ministers had whispered about the danger of revolution behind closed doors, and done what they could to conciliate the trade-union leaders. It was an indication of ruling-class confidence in 1926 that the Cabinet was prepared not only to provoke a strike where one could easily have been avoided, but also, through the militant personality of Winston Churchill, to invent and publicly proclaim a revolutionary conspiracy that had very little basis in fact. The object of the invention – which succeeded – was to terrify the TUC leadership into submission. Such tactics could only be pursued by the Government because, as they well understood, the danger of social revolution was very much more remote in 1926 than it had been seven years earlier.

There can be no doubt about the massive solidarity displayed by the ordinary workers in defence of the miners. One can agree that: 'The strike had tapped the latent enthusiasm of millions of workers. They began to see the possibilities of mass action achieving a solution to suffering and frustrations previously taken for granted.'[56] But to leap from this to assuming that Britain in May 1926 was on the brink of a revolutionary crisis, that the failure of the CP to give a 'correct' lead crippled the imminent revolutionary potential of the strike, reveals a profound failure to comprehend the realities of working-class consciousness. History, the 'orthodox Trotskyist' writers appear to forget, moves not only through the revolutionary party; it moves also in its devious way through the contradictory cross currents of the immensely varied and many-sided consciousness of the working masses. Until this other reality is analysed with all the seriousness that the 'orthodox Trotskyists' devote to their analysis of the internal history of the Comintern and the Party, and with rather more critical control, it is totally impossible even to begin to grasp in any concrete way the dialectical relationship between

45

spontaneity and conscious leadership that lies at the heart of the Leninist theory of the party.[57] This failure to take any serious interest in the real consciousness of real workers stems from, and reinforces, an extreme 'substitutionist' theory of the party. It is the clear implication of 'orthodox Trotskyist' analysis that it is above all the line of the revolutionary party that, if correct, *creates* the revolutionary possibilities. Who needs to know what the mass of the workers thought about it? They were on strike weren't they? – 'objectively' confronting the power of the state. They 'demanded' revolutionary leadership, didn't they? – even if not a whisper of their inarticulate strivings could be heard. A General Strike, after all, *is* a revolutionary situation: elementary, comrade! And so the mechanical application of abstract slogans replaces serious historical analysis.

Liquidating the Minority Movement

The immediate result of the General Strike was a boom in the membership of the CPGB – from 6,000 in April 1926 to 10,730 in October. Over a thousand party members were arrested during the strike itself. The vigour with which party members participated in the strike, their denunciation of the TUC for the betrayal of the miners, and their strenuous efforts to maintain solidarity during the protracted lock-out, all won the CP considerable respect; a large proportion of the membership recruited in 1926 were miners.

In the longer term, however, the results of the strike were as disastrous for the CP as for the working class generally. The perspective held by a minority of the CP, notably Dutt, was that the strike had revolutionized the working class; the 'left' trade union leaders had now been overtaken by the rank-and-file, and were moving steadily rightwards. It followed that the CP should ruthlessly expose the treacherous leaders, and above all the 'pseudo-lefts', and should conduct organized activity within the unions for the election of reliable leaders in their stead.

But most party members rejected these conclusions: the workers were not yet revolutionized, and the united front strategy must continue. Yet clearly the same reliance could no longer be placed on the official leadership, and correspondingly greater emphasis was placed on 'unity from below'. The slogan 'all power to the General Council' was retained, but this was explicitly 'not because we believe in the present leaders of the General Council, but because we believe that a centralized leadership is a necessity of the movement'.[58] Criticism of union leadership was accentuated after the Mond-Turner talks on 'industrial peace' between the General Council and leading employers, with former 'lefts' participating actively. The General Council were now acting openly as agents for the capitalists, and 'it is necessary to state quite frankly that there is no difference between the right-wing and the so-called left-wing on the GC leadership'.[59] A.J.Cook alone was exempt from this charge.

The analysis of the majority did not, however, present a clear guide to action. Since rank-and-file trade unionists still held illusions about their leaders, any unrestrained attack on these leaders would merely isolate the CP and the Minority Movement. In practice the party obtained the worst of both worlds: it attempted to keep attacks on the union bureaucracy within bounds, but was nevertheless assailed for 'disruption'. Even before the General Strike some union leaders had attempted to curb CP activities within their organizations; once the party sharpened its criticisms of union leaders and the Minority Movement began to act as an electoral machine, such attempts became more general. Several unions proscribed communists from office, including membership of TUC delegations. Others prevented branches from affiliating to the Minority Movement or being represented at its conferences. The TUC ended its links with the Russian unions early in 1927 after the latter had criticized its role in the General Strike; at the same time the General Council resolved to withdraw recognition from Trades Councils affiliated to the Minority Movement – a ruling that was overwhelmingly endorsed at the next Congress. The consequence was that the Minority Movement's expansion was contained. The number of delegates at the annual conferences remained only slightly below the peak figure of March 1926; but the number of workers represented was no longer published, and almost certainly fell drastically. Despite vigorous efforts to broaden the Movement's influence (for example, the publication of numerous factory, pit, and industry

47

newspapers) its extension into new unions and new industries was effectively checked; at best the Movement could consolidate its existing organization. Within the party, membership fell by March 1928 to 5,500; losses were particularly heavy in the mining areas, where mushroom recruitment had occurred in 1926. More seriously still, the number of factory groups had fallen below 100.

The insane sectarianism of Stalin's 'third period' completed the process of isolating the British Party – a process initiated by the rightward movement of the trade union leadership after 1926. At the end of 1927 Stalin – who had now ousted Trotsky and was preparing to move against Bukharin – first enunciated the 'left turn' in Comintern policy. Capitalism had now passed through its second period of stabilization into a third period of economic crisis. The class struggle would become accentuated; reformism would finally be revealed as bankrupt; and the reformist leaders of the working class would go over to the bourgeoisie, demonstrating their 'social fascist' character. The united front must therefore be abandoned, and instead the Communist Party must offer the working class independent revolutionary leadership. The new line was endorsed by the Sixth Comintern Congress which met in July 1928. The bulk of the leadership of the CPGB resisted this policy; but at its own Eleventh Congress in November 1929 the supporters of the new line, strongly backed by the Comintern, were victorious, and the Party Executive was purged.

The new line implied a complete reversal in industrial policy: the formation of new unions in place of the existing organizations which were hopelessly dominated by reformist leaders; the creation of factory committees in which non-unionists could take an honourable place, since membership of a reformist union was no virtue; and the establishment of the Minority Movement as the focal point of working-class organization in industry, a revolutionary alternative to the TUC. In practice, even enthusiastic new-liners balked at the implications of Stalin's theses. On dual unionism, the Tenth Party Congress in January 1929 resolved to support breakaway unions where the left wing was threatened by right-wing leaders who were not supported by the majority of the membership. Accordingly, the CP encouraged a breakaway from the Tailors' and Garment Workers' Union in March 1929.

48

The result was disastrous, for the party totally underestimated the support which the Tailors' and Garment Workers' leaders would retain among their members. A second breakaway, the Scottish Mine Workers' Union, was supported a month later. Here there had been a previous breakaway in 1923, in the face of provocation by a right-wing leadership less extreme than occurred in 1929 – and in the face of opposition from the CP, which at that time strongly attacked breakaway unionism. It is doubtful whether the policy of the CP was a major factor behind the formation of the Scottish Mine Workers' Union; and there were no other breakaways in this period. The new line did lead to a more or less adventurist involvement in strikes, together with attempts to form factory committees, notably in textiles; yet CP militants shrank from encouraging non-unionism. Indeed in one major stoppage, at the Austin works in March 1929, CP activists encouraged the largely non-union strikers to join the orthodox trade unions. Nor was there any serious strategy of presenting the Minority Movement as a rival to the TUC, as the RILU had once aspired to rival the Amsterdam International. But in the absence of such a strategy, the end of the united front campaign deprived the Minority Movement of any function; the last annual conference was held in August 1929, and thereafter the Movement was virtually abandoned. When the new line was relaxed from the middle of 1930, the CP turned to other means of industrial intervention.

By the end of the decade the membership of the CPGB had fallen to 3,200, and its industrial influence was at an all-time low. Though only half-heartedly applied, the perspectives of 'class against class' marked the demolition of the framework of organization and activity carefully constructed in association with non-party militants. The isolation of the CP from the bulk of the working class reached its culmination.

A 'serious mass communist party'?

Rejection of the view that the CPGB in the 1920s was operating in a potentially revolutionary situation, on which it failed to capitalize, does not imply accepting Macfarlane's standpoint – i.e. that the Party is to be judged not as a revolutionary party but as a militant reformist organization. As we argued above, the

C   49

only criteria against which to evaluate the performance of the CP in the 1920s are those of the early congresses of the Communist International – i.e. the theory thrown up by the international revolutionary crisis in which the CPGB was formed.

The revolutionary movement, properly so called, consists of those who form the stratum of authentic leaders of working-class militancy – men and women themselves committed to the revolutionary overthrow of capitalism who can command a rank-and-file following in mass industrial or political action. No one, of course, is seeking to infer the attitudes of this rank-and-file from the attitudes of its leaders. Nevertheless, in a society with a large and powerful 'labourist' movement and firmly entrenched reformist ideology, significant sections of the rank-and-file are only likely to turn to revolutionaries for leadership in action when, for one reason or another, their needs and their aspirations come into conflict with traditional labourist organization, or reformist ideology. Short of revolution itself, the measure of success for such a revolutionary stratum is the degree to which it is capable of equipping the rank-and-file, whom it leads in specific struggles, with the revolutionary perspectives within which the leaders themselves view those struggles.

The 'revolutionary *movement*' describes a developing relationship between committed revolutionary leaders and 'spontaneous' rank-and-file militancy. It describes the stratum of revolutionaries *in their relationship with* mass activity. Organize this vanguard into a united revolutionary party, internally constructed on democratic centralist lines, and you have the ideal type of the Leninist party. What is too often forgotten about that ideal type, not just by its opponents, but also by many of its supposed supporters, is that it rests first and foremost on a conception of the relationship between the members of the party and the mass struggle. Just as you cannot have a class without a struggle between classes, so you cannot have a mass revolutionary party without a level of class struggle and of mounting class aspirations that discredits reformist leadership in the eyes of large numbers of workers.

The basic weakness of the CPGB in the 1920s lay in its failure to understand that objective conditions in Britain made it impossible to build what the CI itself defined as a 'serious mass communist party' – one based in a vigorous rank-and-file movement at the point of production, and organized in factory branches. Far from underestimating the possibilities of revolutionary advance in the 1920s, neither the CPGB, nor the CI, understood the full implications of the fact that, in Britain, revolutionary socialist unity represented, not a forward step on a rising tide of struggle, but a retrenchment and consolidation of what forces remained. This is not to say that it was wrong to form the party: in the circumstances of 1919–21 only the formation of a Communist Party could have enabled the vanguard that had been thrown up by the shop stewards' movement to survive the defeat and disintegration of that movement. And, of course, during the 1920s there were mass struggles in which the revolutionaries could attempt to re-establish their relationship with the rank and file – though none with the revolutionary potential of the wartime shop stewards' movement. But they were not sufficiently aware that their task was consolidation, that they were operating on the ebb tide of a major upsurge of working-class combativity. This 'false consciousness' of its situation led the early Communist Party into fundamental strategic errors. Specifically, they were wrong in such a situation to define their *immediate* objective as that of building a mass party.

There are moments, but only moments, when revolutionaries should concentrate their efforts on building a mass party. During the 1905 revolution in Russia Lenin wrote: 'The working class is instinctively, spontaneously social-democratic' [read revolutionary]. And he urged: 'incorporate them in the ranks of the party organizations by hundreds and thousands.' But there was also the Lenin of *What Is To Be Done?*, three years earlier: the Lenin who, rightly, feared the dilution of the party by an influx of workers with a basically 'trade-union consciousness' more than he feared the opposite danger of sectarian isolation. Britain in the 1920s was more like Russia in 1902 than in 1905. This was not the time to attempt to build a mass revolutionary party. The alternative was not to liquidate the party, nor to relapse into a politics of militant reformism (which is what in fact occurred), but rather to consolidate the gains made during the previous

51

decade. This would mean a small cadre party (but not necessarily any smaller than the CPGB was to be, despite its ambitions, in the 1920s), concentrating on internal education, a clear and consistent propaganda informed by revolutionary theory not opportunism, and a real, but relatively limited degree of direct intervention in mass struggle.

Paradoxically, just because the CP, encouraged by the International, set its sights too high in relation to the objectively non-revolutionary situation in which it was operating, it tended to develop a confused and opportunistic style of politics which prevented it from taking full advantage of even those (relatively small) opportunities which were open to the revolutionary movement at the time.

The real cause of the ideological weakness of the British Party, which the 'orthodox Trotskyist' analysis directs to our attention but fails to explain, is to be found in its mistaken attempt to build a mass revolutionary party in a period of working class demoralization and retreat. In the remainder of this study we will examine, in the light of this understanding of the objective situation, the weaknesses of the CP's industrial strategy in the period.

3.
The Communist Party and
Revolutionary Theory

'Without revolutionary theory there can be no revolutionary movement.' Of course it would contradict every principle of marxism to suggest that theory *alone* could generate a revolutionary movement. Yet Lenin's dictum underlines the fact that theoretical clarity is indispensable if a revolutionary party is to exploit successfully whatever possibilities are inherent in the objective situation. In the 1920s, the CPGB was fatally handicapped by theoretical inadequacy and confusion.

As an example it is useful to examine the role of the Minority Movement. In what ways did its formation and operation relate to the perspectives of the CP? At different times at least six distinct definitions were given of the Movement's purpose. Its function was to co-ordinate rank-and-file opposition movements within the unions; to co-ordinate industrial militancy, involving those union leaders who were prepared to fight; to campaign for the organizational restructuring of the trade-union movement, and in particular the TUC; to pursue a programme of transitional demands; to provide a nursery and recruiting ground for potential CP members; or to build revolutionary trade unionism. Quite clearly, such objectives were in many respects divergent and in certain situations might require quite different tactics. Yet it was symptomatic of the party's lack of theoretical clarity that the primary role of the Minority Movement was left blurred. Tom Mann, opening the Movement's founding conference in August 1924, asked the question:

> Why a Minority Movement? Because the trade union movement here and elsewhere has a pretty strong tendency to get into ruts and to get into more and more deep and very deep ruts, and to experience greater and greater difficulties in any attempt to extricate itself.

The Minority Movement was thus intended to extricate trade unionism from deep ruts. This was characteristic of the best and worst in Mann, whose stature within the revolutionary movement rested on his indefatigable activity over half a century rather than on his contribution as a theoretician. But others far closer than Mann to the direction of CP policy were not always much more sophisticated in their formulations of the Movement's role.

A crucial question which was frequently evaded was whether the Movement was to be a revolutionary, or simply a militant reformist organization. Pollitt, its secretary, described the background to the Minority Movement in these terms:

> It was necessary to make a decisive turn towards masswork in the factories, trade unions and working-class organizations, and to try to end the old sectarian traditions of the British revolutionary movement once and for all.
> There emerged from this general policy the idea of trying to organize the Left minority inside the trade unions and the Labour Party in order to fight for the demands of the masses and, at the same time, to attempt to change the whole reformist policy and leadership of the official Labour movement.[60]

This is interpreted by Klugmann as implying that 'what was needed was to rally militants, irrespective of political outlook, for a firm stand against the employers'.[61] The conception of the Minority Movement as a militant reformist body was explicit in Pollitt's speech to the Eighth Party Congress in 1926, when he described it as 'a broad field in which our Party can fight shoulder to shoulder with the increasing numbers of active socialist workers in the trade unions, until experience proves to them that they can fight most effectively as members of the CP'. This was of course in line with the Movement's programme, already detailed: a combination of economic, organizational and broad socialist demands.

On occasion, an even more diffuse image of the Movement was propagated. According to its own constitution, 'the Minority Movement . . . consists of militant members of existing trade unions who aim at making the trade unions real militant organizations for the class struggle'. According to Hardy, its acting secretary in early 1926, 'the NMM is an association of trade unionists who desire to make their unions more efficient and more militant'.[62] A year later, the Movement merely declared that its aim was 'to range all honest workers under our banner'.[63]

Yet elsewhere, it was described not simply as an organization of militant or even socialist workers, but of *revolutionary* trade unionists. The official statement of aims, quoted earlier, committed the Movement 'to organize the working masses . . . for the overthrow of capitalism' as its primary objective. This was in line with the task assigned to British communists by the ECCI in 1923 : 'to convert the revolutionary minority within each industry into a revolutionary majority.'

This duality of interpretation of the Movement's aims had serious implications for the status of its economic programme. Were such demands as a £1 increase in the wages of all workers, together with shorter hours, viewed as objectively attainable in the circumstances of British capitalism in the 1920s? If not, were they explicitly conceived as transitional demands, the struggle for which would raise workers' consciousness beyond mere reformism? Or was the intention merely to allow the 'exposure' of union leaders who inevitably failed to win such concessions from the employers? The programme of the 'Back to the Unions' campaign, which was largely taken over by the Movement, was formulated in the context of the theses of the Second RILU Congress :

> While for the reformist unions the partial demand is an aim in itself, they are for the revolutionary unions just means of consolidating and organizing the masses for the further struggle. The struggle for partial demands does not turn us away from the goal, but brings us nearer to it.

The same argument was rehearsed within the CPGB at the height of the campaign to launch the Minority Movement.[64]

Yet economic demands do not constitute a transitional programme* merely by virtue of being labelled such. At the time, Murphy pointed to the difficulty of creating artificially a

---

* We use the familiar concepts of transitional demands and transitional programme which accurately reflect the content of the resolutions and theses of the early Comintern congresses, even though the actual terminology dates only from the foundation of the Fourth International.

comprehensive programme which could successfully inform the real struggle of the workers.[65] Genuine transitional demands have an organic relationship to the aspirations and experience of the rank and file; yet these inevitably vary from union to union and industry to industry. The Movement's generalized programme, by neglecting such variations, could provide little more than rhetorical slogans. It would be little exaggeration to describe the Movement as a purely *mechanical* application of the theory of the transitional programme: the formulation of artificial economic demands, which could not in themselves form the focus of a genuine working-class struggle, and the even more artificial addition of a series of political objectives unrelated either to the consciousness of trade unionists or to the immediate demands.

The existence of contradictory perspectives for the Minority Movement – militant reformist and revolutionary – and the attempt to bridge the contradiction through a mechanical appeal to the theory of transitional demands, might seem to reflect a similar contradiction inherent in Comintern industrial policy. The Second Comintern Congress, as has been seen, based its theses on the premise of a revolutionary crisis of capitalism, whereas by the Fourth Congress the partial stabilization of capitalism was recognized. Yet throughout the 1920s the RILU – the product of the Second Congress – survived as a cuckoo in the nest of the united front policy. (Hence the enthusiasm with which, when the RILU was barely established, the Comintern sought to merge it with the Amsterdam International.)

The problem of the RILU beset the Minority Movement in microcosm. There are many forms of organization appropriate to the activities of a revolutionary party which can be viewed as natural extensions of the spontaneous industrial struggle. Shop and factory committees, local councils of action, militant fractions in specific industries or unions – all can represent little more than an elaboration of the level of activity and consciousness of rank-and-file trade unionists. The same is true of national campaigns on specific issues. Yet a permanent National Minority Movement covering all industries and unions is manifestly an *artificial* construct. Hence in practice the Movement took on the appearance of (and was at times explicitly defined as) an organized opposition, even when it posed as a mere 'ginger group'; thus even when an unsectarian image was attempted, its very existence was calculated to invite official antagonism. The risk of such antagonism is of course inherent in the work of any revolutionary party; yet it seems questionable tactics to set up a relatively loose front organization which is particularly vulnerable to official reprisals, where the opportunity of mobilizing the rank and file in its defence is limited. Thus in many respects the CP had the worst of both worlds: the Minority Movement's formal autonomy weakened the mechanisms of party control over members' industrial activities; yet its evident subordination to CP policy provided opponents with ready ammunition – the more so given the manifest dishonesty with which party leaders normally insisted that the Movement was wholly independent. Faced with the alternative of providing either a duplication or a dilution of the role of the party, the Minority Movement often succeeded in being both.

Yet if such fundamental contradictions underlay the whole conception of the Minority Movement, why did it achieve at least temporary success? To an important extent, its viability was rooted in features peculiar to the 1920s. A crucial factor was the historical background of rank-and-file movements in the previous decade; the Mining, Metal and Transport Minority Movements were natural successors of this tradition, and the sectional Movements in turn formed the backbone of the National Minority Movement itself. As Pollitt put it:

> The NMM is the natural development of the old Shop Steward and Vigilance Movements. Without their previous existence and experience, it would have been impossible to form one common movement uniting all militant trade unionists, such as the MM is today, even if instructions had been received from ten Internationals.[66]

A further debt to the previous decade was the existence of a large network of highly politicized militants: some in the CP, some on the left of the Labour Party – and some within the leadership of particular unions. This provided an important basis for a united

57

front organization in industry. In addition, the influence of the Russian revolution must be remembered: widespread sympathy for the Soviet experiment could assist the party's own image with non-members; and this in turn could give a CP front organization a non-sectarian appearance (particularly in the absence of rival organizations claiming to be revolutionary). Finally, the financial and organizational resources of the Comintern and the RILU cannot be ignored; without such support it is doubtful how much impact the Movement could have achieved.

The question must in any case be asked: how far *did* the Movement really extend the industrial influence of the CP, or permit intervention in trade-union struggles which would otherwise have been impossible? The Movements in specific industries clearly did have an important function in overcoming sectionalism and uniting militants and opposition forces. But what practical effect did the existence of a *National* Minority Movement have on the industrial struggle? The evidence is sorely lacking.

The problem of the National Minority Movement is ultimately, however, a secondary, organizational question. More fundamental is the issue of the CP's theories of the union bureaucracy and trade-union action as such.

There has never existed a single unambiguous marxist theory of trade unionism.[67] But marxists have long recognized two contradictory tendencies in trade-union action. On the one hand, collective organization represents an important stage in workers' resistance to capitalist exploitation and in the development of consciousness. But since *What Is To Be Done?* marxists have also emphasized the limitations inherent in trade unionism: that in itself it cannot constitute a means to the overthrow of capitalism. There is a natural tendency for the establishment and consolidation of collective bargaining arrangements to become the overriding objective of unionism. This point was clearly recognized by Gramsci in his discussion of trade-union 'legality': established bargaining arrangements with employers are a necessary basis for whatever material gains trade unions are able to win for their members – yet they serve also to reinforce capitalist relations of production.[68] Unions are naturally oriented towards furthering the interests of their own members within the framework of capitalism rather than the interests of the whole class through the abolition of capitalism. As one recent writer has argued: 'as institutions, trade unions do not challenge the existence of society based on a division of classes, they merely express it. . . . By their nature they are tied to capitalism. They can bargain within the society, but not transform it.'[69]

It is true that in favourable circumstances, as Rosa Luxemburg insisted, the struggle for economic reforms can spill over spontaneously into revolutionary action: but 'only in the sultry air of the period of revolution can any partial little conflict between labour and capital grow into a general explosion'.[70] In conditions of stable capitalism, to speak of revolutionary trade unionism involves a contradiction in terms: trade-union action is necessarily structured by the level of consciousness general among the rank and file and by the potential for reform inherent in the objective situation. And even in the course of a revolutionary crisis, trade unionism which becomes revolutionary thereby negates and transcends trade unionism.

In their analysis of union bureaucracy, marxists have commonly emphasized the social and ideological isolation of the fulltime official, together with the pressures which normally make him eager to compromise with employers and the state and reluctant to adopt a posture of greater militancy than is forced on him by the rank and file. To counteract these tendencies a twofold struggle is necessary: to obtain officials with a strong ideological commitment to militancy and a clear understanding of the needs of the situation; *and* to encourage the self-activity of the membership so that its dependence on the leadership is reduced. But it follows from the limitations inherent in trade unionism as such that the struggle of revolutionaries within the unions cannot be substantially more successful than the revolutionary movement at the level of the whole society. The quality and consciousness of union leadership, and the degree of rank-and-file organization and activity, can alter the *terms* of the unions' compromise with capitalism, but not the facts of this compromise. By any absolute standards a trade-union representative, however honest and even revolutionary he may personally be, is in certain objective circumstances bound to 'sell out' if he is to retain his position.

Against the background of marxist theory, what perspectives could have guided the CPGB in the 1920s? Given the special importance of the union bureaucracy during these years, correct policies here were indispensable. Three priorities suggested themselves: the reorganization of trade unionism's formal structure so as to render it more effective in both defensive and offensive struggles; the replacement of leaders so reactionary or incompetent that they would obstruct effective struggle; and pressure on, and co-operation with, more progressive leaders to pursue policies which would raise the consciousness and confidence of the rank and file. But such objectives could properly be pursued only with a full awareness of the severe limitations to which official union action was subject throughout this period. Moreover, the pursuit of such objectives without concurrent attention to the task of mobilizing and politicizing union memberships would seriously distort the direction of party policy. Finally, it was essential that activity within the unions should be organically related to the broader perspectives and policies of the party.

In a sense, all these points were recognized within the CP at the time. Yet it can scarcely be said that pressure at the level of official unionism was effectively integrated with activity at workshop level, or trade-union policies as a whole with the party's broader political agitation and propaganda. There is little evidence of the formulation of coherent perspectives for trade-union work even at the level of the Party leadership, let alone among the membership generally. The inevitable consequences are apparent in some of the major errors of the CP in these years: the repeated call for more powers to the General Council, without proper specification of the necessary safeguards; the failure to warn adequately before the General Strike against the danger of betrayal by the leadership; a voluntaristic conception of union leadership, manifest in an opportunistic attitude to the 'left' leaders and also a personalization of criticisms of leadership actions; and a mechanical approach to internal trade-union work. Part of the tragedy is that the dangers of such policies were from time to time explicitly recognized, but never in such a manner as to correct the Party's overall approach.

As was seen earlier, the demand for a 'general staff of labour' dated back to before the formation of the CP, and was taken up regularly again after 1922. This demand was often expressed in extremely strong terms: 'a definite and even dictatorial power . . . for the purpose of clearing up the mess and imposing some kind of rational system.'[71] In a period of defeat and demoralization, a call for greater centralization in place of the sectionalism of the trade-union movement was obviously correct. Yet it was equally obvious that changes in the formal structure alone would change nothing. As Dutt had previously noted, 'the more powers the General Council has, the less it will be likely to use them'.[72] Even more seriously, greater powers at the centre could be used to suppress militancy and reinforce collaboration with employers. Yet the call for 'more power' often appeared in the party's agitational press without any warning of such danger; and indeed, the party had no coherent strategy for minimizing this danger. A glaring indication of this is the speech of George Hardy, acting secretary of the Minority Movement, to the ECCI plenum in March 1926. Replying to criticism of the slogan 'All power to the General Council', he argued that revolutionary consciousness among the working class would be generated by the very struggle for a powerful General Council; and he concluded:

> Should they use that power wrongly, it only means that we have got another additional task before us of forcing them in the right direction, which direction they will ultimately have to take.[73]

There was in other words no policy for preventing betrayal by the leadership, only for reacting after the event.

At other times, however, the demand was qualified in order to incorporate safeguards. Thus Pollitt, speaking to the Conference of Trades Councils in November 1923, declared:

A real General Council must be established with power to direct the whole movement, and not only with power, but under responsibility to Congress to use that power and direct the movement on the lines laid down each year by Congress. To effect this will mean, not only the extension of the powers of the General Council, but the re-organization of the present trade unions to establish unity on the only basis on which it can be established – the industrial basis – and to prevent the present overlapping and sectionalization that bar the way to united action.[74]

Yet this qualification was in practical terms almost worthless, for revolutionaries had long recognized that industrial unionism was not on the immediate agenda – whereas a powerful General Council *was* intended as an immediate demand. Much the same may be said of the resolution carried at the Minority Movement's founding conference, which is applauded by Pearce:*

It must not be imagined that the increase of the powers of the General Council will have the tendency to make it less reactionary. On the contrary, the tendency will be for it to become even more so. When the employing class realize that the General Council is really the head of the Trade Union movement, much more capitalist 'influence' will be brought to bear on it. . . . The reactionaries desire a General Council which will check and dissipate all advances by the workers. We of the minority movement desire a General Council which will bring into being a bold and audacious General Staff of the Trade Union movement. . . . We can guard against the General Council becoming a machine of the capitalists, and can really evolve from the General Council a Workers' General Staff only by, in the first place and fundamentally, developing a revolutionary class consciousness amongst the Trade Union membership, and in the second place, by so altering the constitution of the General Council as to ensure that those elected thereon have the closest contact with the workers.[75]

---

* Pearce's contention is that the CP expounded a principle line on this question until early 1925, when the Russian leaders' preoccupation with international unity compelled an opportunistic rapprochement with the General Council leadership. In fact, there was no abrupt change of line. Before 1925, detailed consideration of the dangers of reliance on the union bureaucracy was common only in the Party's theoretical journals, and similar analyses can be found after 1925. Articles in the agitational press rarely emphasized these dangers at any time.

The warning of the danger was admirable, but the safeguard proposed was little more than rhetoric. Revolutionary class consciousness was not immediately attainable – this was the whole premise of the united front policy – while there were no immediate prospects of altering the structure of the General Council without the acquiescence of those already in positions of power and influence. The democratization of the TUC was in any case a meaningful demand only in the context of a campaign for the democratization of individual unions. The development of a comprehensive and co-ordinated campaign around this issue would have been of considerable value in the 1920s, but there is no evidence that this was ever treated as a serious priority.

It is true that the demand for a powerful General Council was often associated – particularly in the Minority Movement's programme – with a call for 'unity from below'. This call was taken up vigorously after the summer of 1924, when the formation of factory committees was defined as a major priority by the congresses of Comintern and RILU. Yet this safeguard also was illusory: 'you cannot build factory organizations in empty and depleted workshops, while you have a great reservoir of unemployed workers.' Murphy's assessment of 1922 was not forgotten by the CP leadership in 1924 – the Comintern had to exert considerable effort to persuade the British party that 'the difficulties can and must be overcome'[76] – yet the chimaera of a mass rank-and-file movement was posed as a genuine constraint on the General Council leadership. An increase in the power of the General Council 'involves great possibilities and serious dangers', Pollitt told the first Minority Movement conference. But these dangers were effectively discounted, for the party 'has the greatest faith in the vigilance of the rank and file'. The CP faced a very real dilemma: there were *no* demands open to immediate attainment which would provide guarantees against the General Council's misuse of increased powers. But in place of a clear statement of the dangers in all its agitation and propaganda, the Party all too often lapsed into revolutionary euphoria: 'a powerful mass movement . . . will sweep away the old leadership with its ideas of class peace and limited trade unionism.'[77] This was, of course, to predicate the party's perspectives on the existence of a powerful and independent shop-floor organization which, it was recognized, did not and could not exist.*

The confusion at the time of the General Strike indicated the absence of any coherent theory of trade-union leadership. Lacking an adequate analysis of the structural pressures to which the bureacracy was subject, a voluntaristic interpretation of leadership action was only logical. Thus for Murphy, it was seen, the test of a 'good trade-union leader' was that he should possess 'sufficient character'. This reflected a more general tendency in the Party's assessment of union leadership. According to Gallacher in 1923,

> if we have a fighting policy and the necessary fighting spirit behind it . . . then the one thing needful will be a fighting leadership. . . . Our leaders will have to fight or get out. Some of them we already know will never be any use, but there are others who will fight if they feel that there is some prospect of success.[79]

To suppose that the actions of union officials depend primarily on their *personal* honesty or militancy is of course a negation of marxism; yet this is the doctrine implicit in many pronouncements of the CP in this period. Such voluntarism led, naturally, on the one hand to opportunism, on the other to sectarianism.

The opportunism involved in the Party's attitude to the 'left' union leaders before the General Strike has often been documented. Such opportunism dates from the campaign for the Minority Movement: the success of which, according to Pollitt, demanded the participation of 'the best known and most influ-

---

* The 'orthodox Trotskyist' analysis involves the same assumption. e.g. Pearce:
'Thanks to the policy imposed upon it by Moscow from the spring of 1925 onwards, the MM had done just enough to incur the resentment of the bureaucracy without acquiring the power to fight back effectively.' Yet, regardless of Moscow, such power was objectively unattainable: the NMM was *bound* to incur official resentment and hence its own isolation.[78]

ential leaders'.[80] Yet clearly, as a delegate pointed out at the Seventh Party Congress, this meant a united front with 'well known traitors and fakers': such men as Hicks, the most prominent of the TUC lefts, who had been assailed in the *Workers' Weekly* only a few months earlier for weakness in the face of employer attacks. This was recognized as a serious problem:

> Many revolutionaries will feel unwilling to work alongside officials whom they distrust, often with reason in view of their past records. Nevertheless past records must not be allowed to stand in the way, if a man is ready to fight actively now for a common programme; and we should be ready to welcome such without rancour, so long as they maintain the common fight.[81]

What such an argument ignores is the fact that a man may be 'ready to fight actively' in principle, but in practice succumb to pressures to concede or compromise. Hence no adequate analysis was made or warning given of the *limits* to what could be expected of the left leaders; on the contrary, the party strongly reinforced illusions in 'our friends on the General Council'.[82] Not surprisingly, many party leaders found the betrayal of the General Strike incomprehensible:

> We had men at the head of the General Council who were more afraid of winning than of losing. . . . But why did the better and more virile members of the General Council – those we have called the 'Left Wing' – allow themselves to become involved in their panic?[83]

No answer was suggested to this plaintive query. And indeed none was possible, so long as goodness and virility in a union leader were regarded as sufficient guarantees of militant action.

The mirror-image of this approach was a tendency to hold union leaders personally responsible for defeats. Where concessions and compromises occurred, it was an easy substitute for analysis to blame these on 'reactionaries' or 'pseudo-lefts'. Thus the dominant reaction to Black Friday was the vilification of the Triple Alliance leaders who had failed to support the miners. Williams, secretary of the Transport Workers' Federation, was expelled from the Party. A.J.Cook, then a miners' agent in the Rhondda, was severely attacked for endorsing the terms which ended the lock-out, and resigned from the Party. Criticism was clearly appropriate in such cases; but the manner of the criticism reflected a common failing within the CPGB: the interpretation of leadership acquiescence in defeats solely in terms of individual weakness rather than through a recognition of the pressures towards compromise inherent in the position of any union official.

This personalization of criticism gave the Party's attacks on union leaders – particularly after 1926 – a sectarian quality. Actions which reflected situational pressures were castigated as evidence of personal treachery. Such an approach tended to discredit the CP more than the union leaders; it is well known that an official is admirably placed to appeal to the loyalty of the rank and file when his personal honesty is under attack (even Thomas was able to turn CP attacks to his own advantage). Whether a union official was a right- or left-winger, or even a CP member, effective criticism of his actions had to take account of the pressures to which he was subject. This was a point which Hardy made forcibly to the ECCI:

WHEN OUR PARTY MEMBERS BECOME TRADE UNION OF-FICIALS THERE IS A TENDENCY SOMETIMES TO SAY: 'NOW THAT YOU ARE A COMMUNIST TRADE UNION OFFICIAL YOU MUST DO AS WE LAY DOWN, AND EVERY PART OF OUR POLICY MUST BE PUT INTO OPERATION.'

Comrades, this is an impossible attitude towards trade union officials who are Communists. We must not put the comrades in an impossible position. This attitude will lose influence for the Party. If a comrade's influence as a trade union official is to be of the least practical value, he has to keep himself down on the earth, and be practical. He must deal with the things that the workers want, leading them step by step. As we try to influence the Left trade union official towards Communism, so the Communist union official must try and influence the rank and file and Left officials towards Communism by practical steps.

We have to be flexible with our policy. We have got to be tolerant, because every worker does not reason alike. THE WORKING CLASS ARE NOT NECESSARILY THINKING AS COMMUNISTS SIMPLY BECAUSE THEY ARE PREPARED TO ELECT COMMU-NISTS TO OFFICIAL POSITIONS. A COMMUNIST TRADE UNION OFFICIAL, LOADED UP WITH DETAILS, WHO EVEN DRIFTS AWAY FROM THE PARTY LINE, SHOULD NOT BE RE-GARDED BECAUSE OF THIS ALONE AS A HOPELESS RIGHT WINGER.[84]

Yet how *should* such an official be regarded? Correctly, the Party supported the election of its members to union office: 'if there are still any prejudices against our occupying trade union posts,' Inkpin wrote, 'we have to fight them.'[85] But once CP members achieved office, how far were they expected to accommodate their actions to Party policy – even where this conflicted with the instructions of the union executive or the wishes of its membership? As Hardy insisted, some flexibility was necessary. But there were presumably some limits to the actions permissible if a union official (or, for that matter, a shop steward) were to remain a member of the party; and in certain circumstances party discipline might even require his resignation from union office rather than involvement in a particular act of betrayal. Yet there was never an attempt to specify what these limits and circumstances might be; and this was indeed impossible until the necessary theoretical background was made explicit. It was thus inevitable that 'flexibility' involved an attitude to union officialdom which zigzagged between opportunism and ultra-criticism.

A final indication of the party's unhealthy lack of theoretical perspectives was the *mechanical* approach often adopted towards work in the trade unions. One manifestation of this was the emphasis placed on resolution-mongering and, after 1926 in particular, on electioneering. This trait was particularly evident in Pollitt, who from 1923 was the dominant influence on party policy in industry. His report on the 1922 TUC concluded in stirring fashion:

> The present leaders are powerful because we have scorned to wrestle with them in a practical manner. Alternative policies are what is required. Let us begin now to draft resolutions for next year's Congress.[86]

Drafting resolutions is a necessary part of the activity of any revolutionary; but this can all too easily become an end in itself. It is ironical that Hardy, challenged to justify the Minority Movement's role, cited a 'record of achievement' which was merely a list of militantly worded resolutions carried at the previous

Congresses of the TUC.[87] Equally, organizing support for militant candidates in union elections could also become an end in itself. The correct place of such election campaigns was admirably stated in 1924:

> A small minority of the rank and file are struggling against the passivity and ignorance of the mass of the officials and the mass of the workers. Until the broad popular masses can be reached and quickened through the activity of the left wing, the enlightened union officials are weighted down and cannot move. That being the case, the struggle of the left-wing for leadership is not merely an anti-official struggle. . . . It is a struggle to reach the ordinary worker, to convince him of the need for new policies and new methods of struggle. The business of the MM is not merely to wangle positions for those who support its policy. It is the more fundamental task of capturing the rank and file, of recreating the will to fight.[88]

It may safely be assumed that this argument was not merely for the record: the emphasis reflected the need to combat a real tendency within the CP to treat the 'wangling' of official positions as a short cut to class-conscious trade unionism. After 1926 – particularly with some party members arguing that the working class was already revolutionized – this tendency appears to have become dominant.

'We need *plans* of immediate organized action, definitely related to the existing organized forces of the proletariat, the application of which will force them into *action*. For it is by action that situations are produced which offer the opportunities necessary for a revolutionary change of leadership.' Thus Murphy in 1922.[89] In this respect, he charged, the CP had been notably lacking. There had recently been two important crises: the creation of Councils of Action by the official labour movement in 1920 to prevent British military aggression against Soviet Russia; and the betrayal of the miners on Black Friday. In the first case, communists had participated but had no strategy for escalating working-class action and wresting control of the situation from the official leadership. In the second, the CP had indeed warned in advance that the Triple Alliance would fail; but 'had not, to any great extent, considered or advised the masses what they could do in such an eventuality'. The party had merely *reacted* to events; and Murphy warned against the possibility that 'the next crisis will find us unprepared in a situation akin to its predecessors'.

Murphy's own development in the 1920s was of course a sad one. In the course of the wartime struggles the industrial militants around the SLP developed a highly sophisticated theory of trade unionism, and the writings of Murphy were the most far-reaching of all. Ironically, many of his arguments constitute a devastating critique of the policies later adopted (often with his acquiescence and even enthusiastic support) by the CP. Thus in 1919 he insisted that the proposed 'general staff of labour' was potentially conservative and reactionary, less likely to direct militancy than to constrain it. In 1920 he ridiculed the conception, put forward by some BSP members, of the Trades Councils as potential nuclei of soviets; the whole nature and traditions of Trades Councils prevented them from fulfilling this role. As has been seen, similar insights mark many of his contributions to internal party debate in the early 1920s. Yet as early as 1922 his influential pamphlet *Stop the Retreat* accepted the romanticized notions of the Trades Councils which were to shape an important part of Party industrial strategy for the rest of the decade. As the 1920s continued he was to succumb increasingly to theoretical confusion and wishful thinking. The same trend characterized the Party as a whole.

The Party's lack of theoretical clarity may have been due in part to the change in personnel which followed the process of 'Bolshevization'. The most prominent figures in the party's early years – men like Murphy, Bell and MacManus – had their roots in an organization which consistently emphasized the key importance of revolutionary theory. The SLP's main weakness – its rigidity and sectarianism – had been largely overcome in the course of the wartime shop-floor struggles: by the time its leading industrial militants met Lenin in 1920 they had already overcome their main 'infantile disorders' (at least as far as *trade union* strategy was concerned) and had achieved a remarkable level of theoretical maturity.[90]

Those who most directly controlled CP industrial policy after 1923 – men like Pollitt, Dutt, Gallacher and Campbell – had for the most part lacked so rigorous a theoretical background;

and many had their roots in the opportunist politics of the BSP. The 'practicality' of the BSP had its merits: but the marriage of BSP and SLP failed to engender a higher synthesis, an effective unity of theory and practice. On the contrary: even before 1923 the theoretical acuity of the ex-SLPers was blunted by their immersion in the day-to-day running of Party affairs; but this failing was strongly accentuated after 'Bolshevization'. For the new leadership's background in the practice of the BSP encouraged opportunism as an almost automatic principle of action; and this tendency matched fatefully the opportunities for bureaucracy inherent in the new Party structure. As Pearce puts it, 'the reorganization of 1923 equipped a small, poor party with a top-heavy hierarchy of full-time officials'.[91] Bureaucracy and theoretical creativity accord ill together. As Murphy commented at the time: 'if I were asked what are the principal defects of the Party today, I would answer unhesitatingly, formalism, organizational fetishism, and lack of political training.'[92] Subsequently the *number* of members engaged in Party training courses increased: but the theoretical confusion of the leadership suggests that even when new members were trained, the content of that training left much to be desired.

The Party was hamstrung by contradictory conceptions of trade unionism. The Second Comintern Congress had elaborated, in the context of a period of revolutionary crisis, the possibilities for transcending the reformist limitations normally inherent in trade unionism. Yet even *after* the deflation of the revolutionary crisis, this optimistic evaluation of the possibilities of trade unionism was not wholly discarded. Moreover, once the Minority Movement was established it tended to take on a direction of its own, and pull the (largely unresisting) Party with it. The fact that it was impossible to build the independent rank-and-file organization on which the united front from below had been premised, led not to the abandonment of the NMM, but to an increasing blunting of the Party's theoretical edge. In the argument over whether or not the Party failed to warn of the danger that the left-wing trade union leaders would sell-out in a General Strike, it is possible to select quotations to illustrate either position. This in itself is evidence of the real weakness of the Party in 1924–26:

theoretical confusion. Too often the call was made for a more centralized General Council, without mention of the necessary – but alas unattainable – safeguards. As the strike approached, and the situation became more urgent, this theoretical confusion grew worse, culminating in the quite incomprehensible – facing both ways – article in the *Workers' Weekly* by J.T.Murphy on the very eve of the strike. At the same time there was a tendency to replace structural analyses of the situation of the trade-union bureaucracy with allegations of personal treachery, coupled with misplaced praise for the 'lefts', or silence about their inadequacies. In its effort to identify itself with a mass movement constituted on a profoundly non-revolutionary consciousness, the Party's own theoretical level was degenerating to that of a militant defensive reformism. The understanding of revolutionary theory gained in the struggles that led to the foundation of the Party was being lost. Clear revolutionary propaganda might well have been of more value to the working class movement than the dilution of the Party's ideology in search of mass support.

Conclusions

Our main conclusions may be briefly summarized.

1. It is a common argument that the General Strike created a potentially revolutionary crisis on which the CPGB failed to capitalize because it was misled and corrupted by the Stalinist bloc within the Comintern. This is doubly incorrect. Firstly, it is untrue that the CI was pulling the British Party to the right: almost always the CPGB itself stood to the right of the majority in the International. Thus we insist that it is primarily in terms of the *domestic* situation, rather than the politics of the Comintern, that the history of the early British Party is to be explained.[93] Secondly, given any serious analysis of this domestic situation, it is only in the most abstract sense that 1926 can be described as a moment of revolutionary opportunity.

2. The Party was operating in a profoundly unfavourable situation. The depression years, and the resulting losses in union organization and established wages and conditions, caused widespread resignation and demoralization. The status and influence achieved by reformist leaders in the years of working-class advance were not eroded by the defeats of the 1920s; on the contrary, with the possibility of effective and independent rank-and-file organization largely destroyed, even militant trade unionists felt increasingly dependent on such leaders. Politically, the established institutions of the labour movement exerted a profound influence over the working class, the culmination of almost a century of the hegemony of reformist strategies and ideologies.

3. The Party never came to terms with this situation. It accepted without question the goal set by the euphoric first congresses of the Comintern: the building of a mass revolutionary party. In the vain pursuit of mass membership – and later, more modestly, mass influence – the Party succumbed to an opportunistic style of politics. This degeneration occurred, moreover, *before* Stalin's rise to power and his imposition of similar opportunism on the world Communist movement. In the process, the rich theoretical gains of the British revolutionary movement in the previous decade were lost.

4. The strategy which the objective situation of the 1920s in fact demanded would have been far less ambitious: the consolidation of a revolutionary cadre, the preservation and development of the theoretical achievements of the earlier period of working-class advance. A cadre party placing primary emphasis on the *quality* rather than the quantity of its membership could alone have succeeded in sustaining the British revolutionary tradition in such unfavourable circumstances. (Such a party might, moreover, have proved far more resistant to Stalinism; the British Party was famous – or notorious – for its mindless acquiescence in Stalin's every twist and turn.)

5. Paradoxically, such a strategy need not have required a party any smaller than the actual size of the CPGB during most of the 1920s; nor need its role in the broader labour movement have been any less effective. For in pursuing an over-ambitious conception of its role, the Party failed in almost *every* respect. It began the decade with the heritage of three decades of British revolutionary organization; with a substantial cadre of industrial militants who had won widespread trust and respect as leaders of the wartime struggles; and with considerable advantages as British representatives of Lenin, whose revolution had been hailed far beyond the ranks of committed marxists. But by 1930 the CPGB was little more than an isolated sect, its membership below the level at its foundation, and its influence, though less easily measurable, surely even more catastrophically dissipated.

73

6. Thus the real failure of the CPGB in the 1920s was not that it failed to build a mass alternative to reformism (for that was indeed impossible); it was its inability to establish and sustain a substantial cadre of revolutionaries, and to nurture a significant revolutionary theoretical tradition.

To argue that the attempt to found a mass revolutionary party in the 1920s was mistaken is not to argue that such an attempt is misplaced in the 1970s. In most respects the current position is far more favourable to such an endeavour than was that which faced the Communist Party in its early years. Because of this there are few lessons of direct relevance to our present position that we can learn from the 1920s. Perhaps this, in itself, is the most important lesson. What we build now has not been built before in this country. We are starting from scratch. There is nothing to be gained, and much to be lost, by ransacking the early history of the Communist Party for precedents. If we talk of factory branches, if we talk of a national rank-and-file movement, we must justify these by reference to our own situation – not by false analogies with a mythologized past.

Notes

1. L.J.Macfarlane, *The British Communist Party: Its Origins and Development until 1929*, 1966; R.Martin, *Communism and the British Trade Unions*, 1969
2. J.T.Murphy, *Preparing for Power* (2nd ed) 1972
3. W. Kendall, *The Revolutionary Movement in Britain, 1900–1921*, 1969
4. J.Klugmann, *History of the Communist Party of Great Britain*, Vols I and II, 1969
5. B.Pearce, *The Early Years of the Communist Party of Great Britain*, 1966; M.Woodhouse, 'Marxism and Stalinism in Britain, 1920–26', *Fourth International*, Jul 1967, Feb & Aug 1968, Summer 1969. For further accounts owing much to Pearce and Woodhouse see J.Higgins, 'The Minority Movement', *International Socialism* 45 Nov / Dec 1970, and C.Harman, 'The General Strike', *International Socialism* 48, Jun / Jul 1971
6. J.Higgins, *op cit*, p18
7. For details of the Party's formation see Macfarlane, *op cit* and W.Kendall, *op cit*. But see also the review of the latter by J.Hinton in 'Society for the Study of Labour History', *Bulletin* 19, 1969
8. J.Hinton, *The First Shop Stewards' Movement*, 1973
9. J.Degras (ed), *The Communist International, 1919–1943: Documents,* Vol II, 1923–1928, 1956, p149
10. A.Gleason, *What the Workers Want*, 1920, p184
11. R.Page Arnot, *The Miners: Years of Struggle*, 1953, pp231–32
12. The General Strike is described in detail elsewhere. See, for example, C.Farman, *The General Strike*, 1972
13. H.A.Clegg, A.J.Killick & R.Adams, *Trade Union Officers*, 1961, p38
14. See A.Bullock, *Life and Times of Ernest Bevin*, Vol I, 1960
15. See R.Hyman, *The Workers' Union*, 1971
16. See H.A.Clegg, *General Union*, 1954, and *General Union in a Changing Society*, 1964
17. P.S.Bagwell, *The Railwaymen*, 1963, p412
18. See J.B.Jefferys, *Story of the Engineers*, 1945
19. A. Horner, *Communism and Coal*, 1928, pp204,213–14
20. For these developments see V.L.Allen, 'The Reorganization of the TUC 1918–27', *British Journal of Sociology*, 1960 (also in his *Sociology of Industrial Relations*, 1971) and *Trade Unions and the Government*, 1960

21. J.Degras (ed), *op cit*, Vol I, p148. The details of Comintern policies that follow are taken from the Degras documents
22. See L.J.Macfarlane, *op cit*
23. *Worker*, 18 November 1922
24. See, for example, T.Quelch, *The Call*, 16 October 1919; and the critique of BSP attitudes by J.T.Murphy in *The Socialist*, 6 May 1920
25. *Worker*, 24 March 1923
26. *ibid*, 22 September 1923
27. *Workers' Weekly*, 28 September 1923
28. See W.Gallacher, *Rolling of the Thunder*, 1947, p48
29. *Workers' Weekly*, 4 April 1924
30. J.Degras (ed), *op cit*, Vol II, pp131–32
31. *Communist Review*, October 1924
32. *Workers' Weekly*, 2 January 1925
33. Written 7 and 12 July 1926. Reprinted in *International Socialism* 48, Jun / Jul 1971
34. *Communist Review*, September 1925
35. *Workers' Weekly*, 16 October 1925
36. B.Pearce, *op cit*, p51
37. J.Degras (ed), *op cit*, pp233,235,262
38. *ibid*, p262
39. *ibid*, p299
40. L.J.Macfarlane, *op cit*, p168
41. M.Woodhouse, *op cit*, July 1967, p62
42. L.Trotsky, *Where is Britain Going?*, 1926
43. Contrast Woodhouse, *op cit*, Summer 1969, p35
44. *Worker*, 24 March 1926, 1 May 1926
45. A.Mason, *The General Strike in the North East*, 1970
46. J.Degras (ed), *op cit*, p149
47. L.J.Macfarlane, *op cit*, pp133,135
48. E.Burns, *The General Strike, May 1926: Trades Councils in Action*, 1926
49. R.P.Arnot, *op cit*, pp436–39
50. A.Mason, *op cit*
51. J.Klugmann, *op cit*, Vol II, p162
52. A.Mason, *op cit*, pp17,32, *passim*
53. *cf* J. Hinton, *op cit*
54. D.Baines and R.Bean, 'The General Strike on Merseyside, 1926', in J.R.Harris (ed), *Liverpool and Merseyside: Essays in the Economic and Social History of the Port and its Hinterland*, 1969
55. M.Woodhouse, *op cit*, Summer 1969, p37
56. C.Harman, *op cit*, p26
57. See the excellent exposition of this relationship by Harman in T.Cliff, D.Hallas, C.Harman and L.Trotsky, *Party and Class*, n.d.

58. NMM, *Is Trade Unionism Played Out?*, December 1926
59. NMM, *What is the Minority Movement?*, February 1928
60. H. Pollitt, *Serving my Time*, 1940, p167
61. J. Klugmann, *op cit*, Vol I, p115
62. *Sunday Worker*, 11 April 1926
63. NMM, *Trade Union Leadership*, 1927
64. See for example the article by 'Practicus' in *Workers' Weekly*, 23 November 1923
65. *ibid*, 4 January 1924
66. NMM, *Pollitt's Reply to Citrine*, August 1928
67. For a more detailed discussion of marxist literature on trade unionism see R. Hyman, *Marxism and the Sociology of Trade Unionism*, 1971
68. A. Gramsci, 'Soviets in Italy', *New Left Review* 51, Sep / Oct 1968
69. P. Anderson, 'Limits and Possibilities of Trade Union Action', in R. Blackburn and A. Cockburn (eds), *The Incompatibles*, 1967, pp264–65
70. R. Luxemburg, *The Mass Strike*, 1964, p48
71. *Workers' Weekly*, 28 September 1923
72. *Labour Monthly*, May 1922
73. CPGB, *Orders from Moscow?*, 1926
74. H. Pollitt, *op cit*, pp176–77
75. B. Pearce, *op cit*, pp42–43
76. Report of Piatnitsky discussed by Pollitt, *Workers' Weekly*, 12 December 1924
77. *ibid*, 4 July 1924
78. B. Pearce, *Some Past Rank and File Movements*, p22
79. *Worker*, 22 September 1923
80. *Workers' Weekly*, 21 September 1923
81. *ibid*, 28 September 1923
82. *Sunday Worker*, 23 May 1926 – over a week *after* the end of the General Strike.

     In this context Pearce's argument possesses validity. Lozovsky, who in July 1924 warned against the 'revolutionary phrases of Left-Wing Amsterdamers', was happy by January 1925 to praise 'Purcell's revolutionary speeches'. Dutt, who warned in October 1924 that 'a Left Wing in the class movement must be based upon the class struggle, or it becomes only a manoeuvre to confuse the workers', could write by August 1925 that 'the language of the left trade union leaders is the closest indication of the advance of the British working class to revolution'. Yet at most, the definition of international union unity as a 'revolutionary issue' merely reinforced existing tendencies within the CP.
83. *Workers' Weekly*, 21 May 1926
84. *Orders from Moscow?*, *op cit*

85. *Workers' Weekly*, 1 May 1925
86. *Worker*, 16 September 1922
87. *Workers' Weekly*, 16 April 1926
88. *Worker*, 9 February 1924
89. 'On the Leading Masses', *Communist Review*, February 1922
90. *cf* J. Hinton, *op cit*, Chapter 12
91. B. Pearce, *Early History, op cit*, p60. Pearce goes on, however, to treat the 'bureaucratic degeneration of the CPGB' as a consequence of Stalinism.
92. *Communist Review*, January 1924
93. Our argument derives strong supporting evidence from the history of the Italian Communist Party (PCI) during the same period. Q. Hoare and G. Nowell Smith, in their introduction to their edition of Gramsci's *Prison Notebooks* (1971), insist that '1924–26 was a transitional phase, and it is extremely important to stress the room for manoeuvre still remaining in this period to an individual party such as the PCI'.

    They note that despite the shift to the right in Comintern policy from the spring of 1925, 'there was no corresponding rightward turn in the line of the Italian party, which was to undergo no significant modifications until after Gramsci's arrest. Perhaps part of the reason for the freedom of manoeuvre which this reveals – despite the bolshevization of the communist parties in this same period – was the extremely complex power relations in the Comintern at this time. Zinoviev was President of the International throughout this period; in 1924 he was allied to Stalin and attacking Trotsky for his 'anti-peasant' policies; by 1926 he was allied to Trotsky and attacking Stalin and Bukharin for their 'pro-peasant' policies. From early in 1925 a Bukharinist Right began to emerge within the Comintern. . . . The upshot of this complex situation seems to have been that Zinoviev on the one hand and the Bukharinist Right on the other effectively cancelled each other out for this period, with the result that it was possible for 'leftist' policies in countries like Germany and Italy to coexist with 'rightist' policies in countries like China, the United States, Britain or Yugoslavia. In each case, the determining factors were national rather than international.'

Pluto  **Press**

For a list of
books and pamphlets available
write to:

Unit 10 Spencer Court,
7 Chalcot Road, London NW1 8LH

Carter L. Goodrich

The Frontier of Control
with a new foreword and notes by Richard Hyman

A new edition of a classic on the movement for workers'
control in Britain first published in 1920.

'The Frontier of Control' records the struggle between
management and workers for control inside the factories.

It shows how strong workers are when they are acting for
themselves; and how weak when they are not.

The book was written at a time when Britain was closer to
revolution than at any other time in modern history; when the
armed forces were sullen and mutinous, the police were actively
organizing to form a union; and when workers were taking
'direct action' to press their claim.

Paperback / hardback

Pluto Press, Unit 10 Spencer Court,
7 Chalcot Road, London NW1 8LH